Unlocking Capital

The Power of Bonds in Project Finance

by

H. Burak Erten

Table of Contents

Introduction

At the heart of global economic development lies the crucial role of financing large-scale projects. Among the myriad of financial tools available, bond issuance stands out as a robust mechanism for project sponsors, bankers, insurance professionals, and professionals in the capital markets to leverage in the pursuit of transforming visions into tangible realities. This book delves into the intricate world of bond financing, offering an in-depth exploration designed to fortify the expertise of bankers, project sponsors, insurance specialists, and others in related fields. An invaluable resource for both seasoned practitioners and newcomers, the contents herein serve educational purposes for students and academics alike.

The endeavour to understand bond issuances and their application within project finance is no trivial task. It requires a nuanced grasp of various elements, such as bond types, the issuance process, the players involved, risk management, regulatory considerations, and market dynamics. A logical starting point is to first comprehend the foundational elements that constitute a bond, its lifecycle, and its functional role in the larger framework of financing projects.

Subsequent chapters progressively delve into the specifics of bond types—each with unique characteristics and applications. We proceed to dissect the anatomy of a bond to familiarize readers with essential terminology and features. Thereafter, the book methodically guides readers through the issuance process, shedding light on the players who animate the bond ecosystem, and the significance of credit ratings in such undertakings.

Risk, being an inherent element of financial transactions, is addressed comprehensively, allowing for an understanding of how it informs the structure of bond financing and the subsequent pricing mechanisms. We journey through the essentials of domestic and international regulations to ensure compliance, while also considering the environmental, social, and governance (ESG) impacts that increasingly inform investment decisions.

As we look towards the innovational horizon, the book does not shy away from discussing novel bond structures and the technological advancements shaping the future of bond financing. Indeed, staying abreast of the evolution in digital bond issuance, emerging market trends, and strategic marketing for bond offerings is pivotal for anyone involved in project finance.

By the end of this comprehensive guide, readers will have garnered the knowledge necessary to navigate the complexities of bond financing, equipped with strategies for mitigating risks, adhering to regulatory frameworks, and capitalizing on technological advancements. This book serves as a testament to our commitment to providing a clear, systematic, and scientifically grounded treatise on the mechanics of bond issuance, tailored to meet the needs of professionals committed to project finance.

Chapter 1:
Fundamentals of Project Finance

The financing of large-scale projects presents a myriad of challenges, not least of which is securing sufficient capital. This is where the intricate world of project finance bonds comes to the forefront. Bonds serve as a critical vehicle for raising the long-term capital needed to fund infrastructure, energy, and various other large-scale projects. Understanding their role and characteristics is vital for anyone involved in project-based financing.

The Role of Bonds in Project Finance

Bonds are a cornerstone in project finance, offering a means to leverage large sums of money through debt securities. These debt instruments are particularly appealing as they allow for the borrowing of capital while spreading the risk among a wide base of investors. As lenders to the project, bondholders have a vested interest in the successful completion and operation of the project, as it bears directly on their returns (Esty, 2004).

Through the issuance of bonds, project sponsors can access a broad pool of investors from the capital markets, thus diversifying their funding sources beyond the traditional loans from financial institutions. This not only balances risk but may also offer more favourable terms and conditions compared to other forms of debt.

Characteristics of Project Finance Bonds

Project finance bonds exhibit unique characteristics differentiating them from corporate bonds or other traditional forms of financing. They are secured against the project's assets and cash flows rather than the broader creditworthiness of the sponsor. The earmarking of revenue from the project itself to service debt obligations implies that assessing project viability and risk is paramount (Yescombe, 2002). As these bonds are often tied to projects with long lifecycles, such as infrastructure development, they typically exhibit longer maturities and may include features to provide flexibility, such as call or put options.

Bond Market Overview for Project Sponsors

An understanding of the bond market and its mechanisms is essential for project sponsors. By grasping fundamental concepts such as bond pricing, yield curves, and the impact of credit ratings, sponsors can make informed decisions about engaging with the bond market. Market sentiment and economic conditions play significant roles in determining the cost of borrowing and the timing of bond issuances. Project sponsors must keep abreast of these factors to optimize their approach to financing (Fabozzi, 2012).

In summary, project finance bonds are a sophisticated asset class that provides essential capital for large projects. They offer an alignment of interests between the project and its financiers and necessitate a detailed understanding of the underlying project risks. As this chapter lays the groundwork, subsequent chapters delve deeper into the specifics of bond types, features, issuance processes, and strategies critical to effective project finance.

The Role of Bonds in Project Finance

Bonds serve as a critical instrument in project finance, providing long-term, fixed-income investment opportunities for investors and a source of capital for project sponsors. In the realm of project finance, bonds offer a unique advantage due to their ability to raise large amounts of capital with relatively predictable cash flows and structured repayment terms (Fabozzi et al., 2008).

Given the typically substantial initial outlay and the long gestation period of infrastructure and development projects, bonds present an attractive financing solution. They are capable of matching the long-term nature of such investments, which is often a challenge for more traditional forms of debt financing with shorter tenures. A bond's structure, incorporating fixed coupon payments and a defined maturity date, aligns well with the project's timeline, which in turn affords a measure of stability and predictability for project sponsors and investors alike.

Risk mitigation is another significant aspect where bonds come into play in project finance. By issuing bonds, project sponsors can transfer some of the project risk to the bondholders. The categorization of these bonds, ranging from senior, which enjoy a higher claim to a project's assets and cash flows, to subordinate bonds, reflects the differing levels of risk absorption (Esty, 2004). The incorporation of credit enhancements, such as third-party guarantees or letters of credit, also serves to improve the bond's creditworthiness and, by extension, its attractiveness to potential investors.

Bonds in project finance can be issued in various forms, with each type designed to cater to specific project characteristics or investor risk appetites. The diversity within bond structuring allows for tailored financial solutions that can accommodate the particularities of each project, ranging from revenue bonds tied to the project's future earnings, to more creative constructs like green bonds that finance projects with an environmental benefit (Kidney et al., 2015).

Overall, bonds in project finance play a multifaceted role, offering project sponsors an alternative or complement to bank lending, while providing investors with investment opportunities in substantial infrastructure projects with a transparent risk profile. As project finance continues to evolve, the significance of bonds and the innovation within this space play a pivotal role in shaping the future landscape of infrastructure funding and development.

Characteristics of Project Finance Bonds

Project finance bonds are a distinct class of investment vehicles, serving as a critical instrument for raising long-term capital for large-scale infrastructure and industrial projects. They differ from traditional corporate bonds in several key aspects, primarily due to the unique nature of project financing. In this section, we'll explore these characteristics in detail, providing professionals in banking, insurance, and capital markets with a clear understanding of project finance bonds.

Firstly, project finance bonds are commonly issued by a special purpose vehicle (SPV), which is a legally independent company created specifically for the project. The SPV serves to isolate the financial and operational risks of the project from the sponsors' balance sheets (Esty, 2004). This structure is primarily used to secure creditors by ring-fencing the project assets and revenue streams, ensuring that they are not affected by the financial status of the project sponsors.

The repayment of project finance bonds is predominantly reliant on the future cash flows generated by the project, rather than on the financial strength of the issuing entity or its sponsors. This is a fundamental difference from corporate bonds, where repayment is backed by the broader creditworthiness of the issuing corporation. As a result, the evaluation and pricing of project finance bonds are heavily dependent on detailed cash flow projections and the underlying risks of the project itself, including construction, operational, market, and environmental risks (Yescombe, 2002).

Another defining characteristic is the long-term nature of project finance bonds. Infrastructure and industrial projects typically have extended periods of construction and operation, necessitating the need for long-dated debt that matches the expected cash flow profile. These bonds often have maturities ranging from 10 to 30 years or even longer, which aligns with the lifecycle of the project (Nevitt & Fabozzi, 2000). The alignment of the bond's maturity with the project's life can offer more predictable financing costs and can potentially reduce the refinancing risks associated with short-term debt.

Furthermore, project finance bonds often incorporate covenants and credit enhancement features designed to manage and mitigate risk. Such covenants may restrict the actions of the SPV in order to protect bondholder interests, while credit enhancements might include reserve funds, guarantees, or insurance policies, which can improve the credit profile of the bonds and potentially lower the financing costs (Fabozzi et al., 2008).

In conclusion, the characteristics of project finance bonds—such as the use of an SPV, cash flow-based repayment, long maturity periods, and tailored covenants and credit enhancements—make them a unique and vital tool for financing large-scale projects. These features are designed to address the particular risks and challenges associated with project finance, thereby providing bondholders with a level of reassurance while enabling project sponsors to secure the necessary capital for development.

Bond Market Overview for Project Sponsors

Understanding the bond market is vital for project sponsors who aim to use this arena for project finance. The bond market, also known as the debt, credit, or fixed-income market, is a financial market where participants can issue new debt, known as the primary market, or buy and sell debt securities, known as the secondary market. It primarily includes government and corporate bonds, and it is where project finance bonds are transacted.

Project finance bonds are a form of fixed-income securities that are issued to finance large infrastructure and industrial projects. One key aspect that project sponsors must consider is the size and liquidity of the bond market. Despite fluctuations, the bond market is generally characterized by its depth, with a vast array of institutional investors such as pension funds, mutual funds, and insurance companies providing capital (Fabozzi, 2018).

Risk mitigation is one of the main concerns in the bond market, and project sponsors must be aware of various strategies to make their bond issuance more attractive. Credit enhancements such as surety bonds, letters of credit, insurance policies, or the structuring of reserve funds can be employed to attain a better credit rating and, therefore, a reduced cost of capital (Kraemer & Gurwit, 2019). Interest rates and credit spreads are other critical factors for project sponsors to monitor as they influence the pricing of the bonds in the market.

For a project sponsor, it's of paramount importance to understand the regulatory environment in which the bond issuance operates. In the United States, this is predominantly governed by the Securities and Exchange Commission (SEC) and the Municipal Securities Rulemaking Board (MSRB) (Frankel, 2020). Regulations not only protect investors but also impose certain reporting and disclosure requirements on issuers.

Market dynamics within the bond market can fluctuate due to macroeconomic factors such as interest rate changes, inflation expectations, and global economic health. A project sponsor must stay informed of market conditions to time their entry for bond issuance favorably. This requires a close relationship with financial advisors and underwriters who can provide guidance on when to enter the market and at what terms.

In conclusion, the intricacies of the bond market hold significant implications for project finance. Project sponsors need to have a comprehensive understanding of the bond market's size, liquidity, risk mitigation strategies, regulatory framework, and prevailing market dynamics to successfully raise capital for their projects. The knowledge of these elements enables better decision-making and can lead to a more cost-effective and efficient bond issuance process.

Chapter 2:
Types of Bonds in Project Finance

Having delved into the foundational concepts of project finance and the role that bonds play in the sector in the previous chapter, we now turn our attention to the various types of bonds that financiers may leverage to support large-scale projects. Bonds, in their essence, are debt instruments providing the borrower with external funds to finance long-term investments. Different bonds suit different aspects of project finance depending on the project's nature, scale, geographic location, and underlying revenue streams.

Corporate Bonds

Corporate bonds are issued by companies seeking to raise capital for expansion, acquisitions, or other significant investments, including project finance. These bonds are typically backed by the general creditworthiness and reputation of the issuer rather than a specific source of revenue. Investors are rewarded with interest payments at fixed intervals, and the bond's face value is repaid upon maturity (Kidwell et al., 2002). The risk associated with corporate bonds varies based on the issuing entity's financial stability, which is often reflected in credit ratings assigned by established agencies.

Municipal Bonds

Municipal bonds, or "munis," are debt obligations issued by local or state governments to fund public projects such as schools, highways, or hospitals (Brigham & Ehrhardt, 2016). These bonds can be appealing to investors due to potential tax exemptions on interest income and often exhibit lower default risks than corporate bonds. They are integral to project finance within the scope of public infrastructure development and urban planning. The two primary types of municipal bonds are discussed in the following sections.

Revenue Bonds

Revenue bonds are a subtype of municipal bonds secured by the revenues generated from the project they are intended to fund. Unlike general obligation bonds, they are not backed by the issuer's taxing power. For example, if a revenue bond is issued to fund a toll bridge, the toll collections would be used to pay bondholders. Due to the direct link to project performance, revenue bond investors take on more risk, which may yield higher returns if the project succeeds (Fabozzi et al., 2014).

General Obligation Bonds

General obligation bonds represent another form of municipal bonds with repayment secured by the full faith and credit of the issuing municipality. This means that the issuer can use tax revenues or other resources to repay bondholders. Consequently, general obligation bonds generally carry less risk than revenue bonds, attracting investors seeking more secure investment opportunities within project finance.

Convertible Bonds

Convertible bonds are a hybrid type of corporate bond offering both debt and equity features. These bonds provide investors with the right, but not the obligation, to convert the bond into a predetermined number of shares in the issuing company. Given their equity component, convertible bonds can be attractive to investors who anticipate the issuing company's share price will increase over the term of the bond (Damodaran, 2001). This characteristic can make convertible bonds a useful tool for companies involved in project finance who wish to capitalize on their growth potential while retaining favorable borrowing conditions.

In conclusion, understanding the diverse types of bonds available is crucial for professionals involved in project finance. Each type comes with its own set of features, risks, and benefits that must be carefully considered in conjunction with the specific needs and circumstances of the project. The next chapter will delve into the anatomy of a bond, providing valuable insight into their key features and life cycle.

Corporate Bonds

In the context of project finance, corporate bonds represent a critical channel through which businesses can raise capital for large-scale projects. Unlike equity, which implies ownership, corporate bonds are a form of debt, meaning that the issuer promises to pay back the borrowed funds plus interest over time to the bondholders. This distinction proves particularly significant because it allows companies to undertake substantial projects without diluting shareholders' interests.

Corporate bonds typically carry a fixed interest rate, known as the coupon rate, and have a predetermined maturity date by which the principal, or face value, is to be repaid (Fabozzi et al., 2008). They are issued by corporations and are used to finance a variety of business activities, including capital expenditures, refinancing of existing debt, and mergers and acquisitions.

When it comes to project finance, corporate bonds may be secured or unsecured. Secured bonds offer bondholders a claim on specific assets of the company as collateral if the firm defaults on the bond payments, thereby reducing the risk for investors. Unsecured corporate bonds, known as debentures, do not provide collateral, making them more risky for bondholders but often offering a higher return to compensate for this increased risk (Baker & Martin, 2011).

One of the key considerations in using corporate bonds for project finance is the creditworthiness of the issuing corporation. The credit rating, a measure typically provided by rating agencies, influences both the interest rate the company must pay and the appetite of the market for its bonds. Firms with higher credit ratings will generally be able to borrow at lower costs than those with lower credit ratings (Moody's Investors Service, 2019).

Risk mitigation strategies are also fundamental when considering corporate bonds in project finance. Issuers often utilize covenants, which are contractual provisions that can proclaim certain actions the issuer must perform (affirmative covenants) or restrict particular activities (negative covenants), to offer some protection to investors (Reed & Smith, 2010). These covenants are designed to preserve the project's integrity and financial viability, providing bondholders with greater confidence in the project's ability to generate sufficient revenue to meet its debt obligations.

In summary, corporate bonds present a viable option for funding project finance, offering a means by which companies can leverage their credit standing and operational capacity to raise substantial funds. However, careful attention must be directed towards the structure and terms of the bonds to ensure they align with the project's needs and the investors' requirements.

Municipal Bonds

Municipal bonds, frequently termed as "munis," are a crucial category of debt securities utilized primarily by state, local governments, and other municipal entities to raise capital for public projects such as roads, schools, and infrastructure improvements, which are vital to community development and enhancement (Fabozzi et al., 2020).

Unique in their position within the project finance landscape, municipal bonds are noteworthy for their tax-exempt status. The interest earned by investors on most municipal bonds is exempt from federal income taxes, and often from state and local taxes, particularly if the investor resides in the state where the bond is issued.

Given that municipal bonds are issued by a host of public entities, such as states, cities, counties, and other governmental subdivisions, they carry diverse risk profiles often correlated to the financial stability and revenue-generating potential of the issuing entity. As project sponsors, bankers, and other stakeholders delve into the intricacies of using municipal bonds for financing initiatives, they must consider the two primary types of municipal bonds: general obligation bonds and revenue bonds (Feldstein & Fabozzi, 2011). General obligation bonds are supported by the full faith and credit of the issuer, with repayment assured through taxing power. In contrast, revenue bonds are repaid from the income generated by the specific project they fund, making them inherently riskier, as their solvency hinges on the project's financial performance.

The issuance process of municipal bonds involves a preliminary official statement (POS) which lays out the project details, financials, and the terms of the bond issuance. The POS plays a crucial role in marketing the bonds to potential investors. Given their complexity and implications for public policy, municipal bond issuances generally undergo stringent scrutiny and must adhere to the legal standards stipulated by the Securities and Exchange Commission (SEC) and the Municipal Securities Rulemaking Board (MSRB) (Feldstein & Fabozzi, 2011).

Municipal bonds can offer a range of maturities, typically from short-term notes of less than one year to long-term bonds that can extend for periods of over 30 years, accommodating various financing strategies and needs of municipal entities. The inherent attractiveness of municipal bonds, particularly those that are tax-exempt, lies in their lower yields relative to taxable bonds, which often results in significant tax savings for higher-income investors. This tax advantage can be a compelling incentive for both retail and institutional investors to include municipal bonds in their investment portfolios.

Given their mission-critical nature for funding essential public services and infrastructure, municipal bonds carry an element of social responsibility, aligning investor returns with community development. As such, they are often highlighted within discussions of environmental, social, and governance (ESG) criteria in investment decision-making.

In sum, municipal bonds represent a distinctive vehicle within project finance, one that balances the needs of public entities to fund crucial projects with investor appetite for tax-advantaged, socially responsible investment opportunities. For capital market professionals, understanding the structure, benefits, and potential risks of municipal bonds is paramount to guiding investment strategies and fostering community growth (Fabozzi et al., 2020).

Revenue Bonds

In the realm of project finance, Revenue Bonds stand as a pivotal instrument for funding a myriad of public and private initiatives. Unlike general obligation bonds, which rely on the issuer's taxing power to guarantee repayment, Revenue Bonds are secured by the future cash flows generated from the project or asset they finance (Fabozzi, 2015). This bond type is frequently employed in sectors where the financed asset can produce a stream of income, such as utilities, toll roads, hospitals, or housing developments.

The income stream generated by the project directly correlates with the bond's revenue, constituting the primary source for interest and principal payments. Therefore, the creditworthiness of Revenue

Bonds is intrinsically tied to the financial success of the underlying project, rather than the credit of the municipality or corporate entity that issues them. This linkage necessitates a scrupulous analysis of the projected cash flows and a thorough understanding of the operational risks associated with the project (Esty, 2004).

For bankers, investors, and other stakeholders, this form of bond entails a closer inspection of the project's feasibility and potential profitability. When compared to general obligation bonds, the risk of default can be higher with Revenue Bonds if the project underperforms. To mitigate such risks, bond covenants and reserve funds are often put in place as safety nets, and additional credit enhancements might be sought. Insurance, for instance, can be acquired to bolster the bond's attractiveness and reassure investors about the timely servicing of debt.

Revenue Bonds can be structured to align with different revenue scenarios of the project. They may feature a fixed or variable coupon rate and can be tailored to match the project's expected cash flow timeline, offering flexibility in terms of repayment schedules. Issuers must also consider the regulatory environment in which the bonds are offered, as it may influence permissible bond structures, disclosure requirements, and the tax treatment of interest payments to investors (Schwarcz, 2002).

In conclusion, Revenue Bonds play a substantial role as a funding mechanism within project finance. Their unique reliance on the cash flows of the project they finance necessitates an in-depth appraisal of the project's economic viability. Therefore, a collaborative effort among project sponsors, bankers, and advisors is critical to structure these bonds adequately, manage potential risks effectively, and ensure the alignment of the financial obligations with the anticipated revenue generation of the undertaking.

General Obligation Bonds

In the realm of project finance, *General Obligation Bonds* (GO Bonds) represent a fundamental type for financing a wide array of public projects. Unlike revenue bonds that are repaid from specific income streams generated by a project, GO Bonds are secured by the full faith and credit of an issuing municipality, which pledges to leverage its taxing power to repay bondholders. Essentially, these bonds are backed by the issuing authority's ability to tax its residents (Zimmerman & Harris, 2018).

Project sponsors and capital market participants must note that GO Bonds typically require voter approval before they can be issued. This democratic aspect means that the bonds are often earmarked for projects that the public deems necessary or beneficial, such as infrastructure improvements, school renovations, and other community-centric services. Additionally, the credit rating of general obligation bonds tends to be higher than revenue bonds, as the entire financial weight of the issuer supports the debt service, minimizing default risk (Fabozzi, 2020).

Given the lower risk profile associated with GO Bonds, they often come with more favourable interest rates from an issuer perspective, which can be a compelling incentive for project sponsors considering different financing options. However, the trade-off lies in the constraints placed upon the funding. Since the proceeds come from taxpayers, there is heightened scrutiny over how funds are allocated, and projects financed with GO Bonds may be subject to specific regulations and guidelines to ensure they serve the public interest.

Bankers and financial advisors involved in structuring GO Bonds must understand the legal implications that come with this type of financing. For instance, the issuer's annual budget and financial resources must accommodate debt service without endangering the entity's solvency. Furthermore, it is essential to understand the potential impact of macroeconomic changes, such as tax base fluctuations, which may affect the issuer's ability to meet its obligations.

For those in the insurance sector, the solid credit foundation of General Obligation Bonds often means that credit enhancement through bond insurance may not be as critical as it is for other bond types, although it can still be utilized to improve the debt's marketability and reduce borrowing costs.

Lastly, capital market professionals should be aware that successful issuance of GO Bonds involves a robust marketing strategy that communicates the value and purpose of the financed projects to voters and investors effectively (Ehlers & Schich, 2019). In summary, General Obligation Bonds present a stable mechanism for funding projects with the backing of an issuing authority's creditworthiness and an ethical alignment with community interests.

Convertible Bonds

Within the varied landscape of bonds used in project finance, convertible bonds stand out as a uniquely flexible instrument that caters to both the interests of investors seeking the potential for equity appreciation and project sponsors requiring cost-efficient capital. As hybrid securities, convertible bonds combine features of both debt and equity, offering investors the option to convert their bonds into a predetermined number of equity shares of the issuing company at specific times during the bond's life, typically at the discretion of the bondholder.

For project sponsors, the issuance of convertible bonds can be particularly attractive because it initially places less burden on cash flow due to potentially lower interest rates compared to traditional bonds (Krishnamurti & Vishwanath, 2013). This cost-efficiency arises from the bond's equity conversion feature, which investors may value, therefore accepting a lower coupon rate. However, this comes with the caveat of potential dilution of ownership if the bonds are converted into equity.

The mechanism of conversion is usually determined at the time of issuance and is defined by a conversion rate, which specifies the amount of equity an investor receives upon conversion. The conversion rate can be subject to adjustments to protect investors from events like equity dilution resulting from corporate actions, such as mergers or stock splits (Brigham & Ehrhardt, 2016).

Risk mitigation strategies for convertible bonds necessitate careful structuring. As these bonds straddle the line between debt and equity, project sponsors must be attentive to the balance between inviting investment and maintaining control of the venture. Convertibles may include provisions to protect both the issuer and investor, such as call provisions, affording the issuer the right to redeem the bonds before maturity typically to limit equity dilution, and put provisions, allowing investors to sell the bond back to the issuer at a predetermined price.

Moreover, the strategic use of convertible bonds in project finance can align sponsor and investor interests when the project's performance directly influences the underlying value of the conversion option. As the project succeeds and the company's stock value increases, the incentive for bondholders to convert their debt into equity grows, potentially reducing the debt on the company's balance sheet and aligning the interests of bondholders with shareholders (Fabozzi, Davis, & Choudhry, 2006).

Nevertheless, the conversion feature's pricing requires intricate financial modelling to ensure fair valuation that respects the risk-return trade-off. This is critical, as mispricing can lead to unfavourable terms for either the sponsor or the investors, potentially undermining the financing strategy.

In conclusion, convertible bonds represent a distinctive and multifaceted instrument in the realm of project finance. Their dual nature offers a means to strike a dynamic balance between present capital needs and future growth prospects, embedding a possible equity upside for investors in the form of conversion rights. When optimally structured, convertible bonds can address capital requirements while offering a pathway to equity participation, which can be particularly advantageous in long-term, capital-intensive projects where initial profitability may be uncertain or delayed.

Chapter 3:
The Anatomy of a Bond

The intricate structure of a bond is pivotal for bankers, project sponsors, insurance professionals, and capital market participants to comprehend. To appreciate the multifaceted nature of this financial instrument, one must meticulously dissect its components and understand each aspect's role in the overarching mechanism of bond financing. This chapter aims to elucidate the key features, terminology, and lifecycle of bonds which are integral to the understanding and utilization of bonds in finance projects, as well as to identify the risk mitigation strategies that are associated with them.

Key Features and Terminology

In the realm of bonds, several fundamental terms and concepts form the bedrock of this financial tool. Crucial to the valuation and trading of bonds, these attributes determine the income stream and risk profile that bonds offer to investors.

Coupon Rates indicate the interest rate that the bond issuer agrees to pay its bondholders. This rate is generally presented as a percentage of the bond's face value, and payments are usually made semi-annually. The coupon rate is concurrent with the creditworthiness of the issuer and the prevailing interest rates in the market (Fabozzi, 2018).

Maturity Dates are the predefined dates on which the principal amount, also known as the face value of the bond, is scheduled to be paid back to the bondholders. Bonds can have varying lengths of time to maturity, from short-term notes of a few months to long-term bonds that mature over several decades (Tuckman & Serrat, 2020).

Face Values refer to the principal amount of the bond that is repaid at maturity. This is also often called the 'par' value of the bond. The face value is important as it determines the actual amount of cash the bond will yield for investors under its term, excluding any effects from market price fluctuations.

The Lifecycle of Bonds

The lifecycle of a bond begins with its issuance and concludes with its maturity. Upon issuance, the bond enters the primary market where it is purchased by investors. Following the initial sale, the bond may be traded among investors in the secondary market. The life of the bond comprises a series of interest payments based on the coupon rate, culminating in the repayment of the face value at maturity (Fabozzi, 2018).

Understanding the lifecycle is crucial for investors and issuers as it influences risk assessment, pricing strategies, and overall financial planning. The bond's journey from issuance to maturity is shaped by numerous market factors, regulatory considerations, and issuer-specific events which can affect the bond's performance and perceived risk.

In conclusion, the structure of a bond is composed of its fundamental features: coupon rates, maturity dates, and face values. These elements, along with the lifecycle stages of issuance, trading, and maturity, form what can be considered the 'anatomy' of a bond. As the spine of the bond's framework, these components must be meticulously considered by professionals engaged in project finance, as they directly influence the investment's attractiveness and compatibility with strategic financing goals.

Key Features and Terminology

Understanding the anatomy of a bond is crucial for professionals involved in project finance. Bonds, as complex financial instruments, have distinct features that are pivotal when structuring a deal. This knowledge aids in aligning the financial product with the project's cash flow needs and risk appetite. We'll dissect the essential aspects and the vocabulary integral to bonds within the realm of project finance.

Coupon Rate: The coupon rate is the interest a bond pays, typically conveyed as an annual percentage of its par or face value. This rate affects a bond's market price and yield, where a higher coupon generally indicates a higher yield, provided market rates remain constant (Fabozzi, 2018). The coupon can be either fixed, changing little over the bond's life, or variable, adjusting at intervals alongside market rates (Frank et al., 2009).

Maturity Date: This is the date on which the principal amount of a bond is due to be repaid to the bondholder. Bonds can have short, medium, or long-term maturities, affecting the bond's interest rate sensitivity and investment risk (Fabozzi, 2018).

Face Value: Also known as the par value, this is the amount the issuer agrees to repay the bondholder at maturity. It is also the base amount on which coupon interest is calculated (Fabozzi, 2018).

In addition to these core features, the terminology used in the context of bonds includes:

- **Yield:** A measure of return on a bond, factoring in the coupon rate and price changes.

- **Yield to Maturity (YTM):** An estimation of all possible yields realized if the bond is held until maturity.

- **Principal:** The face amount of the bond, which represents the initial investment.

- **Issuer:** The entity that creates the bond to raise funds, which could be a corporation, a government body, or a municipality.

Understanding these key features and terms lays a foundation for the subsequent stages of bond creation and lifecycle, as well as for risk assessment, pricing, and compliance (Fabozzi, 2018; Frank et al., 2009).

Coupon Rates As we peel back the layers of bond anatomy to gauge the intrinsic elements that influence investor demand and issuer obligation, one cannot overlook the critical aspect of coupon rates. Coupon rates, also referred to simply as 'coupons', are the periodic interest payments made to bondholders and serve as a pivotal metric reflecting not only the cost of borrowing for the issuer but also the income generated for the investor (Fabozzi, 2012). The coupon rate is typically presented as a percentage of the face value of the bond and is a fixed figure etched into the bond's terms at the time of issuance.

For project finance, which often entails substantial capital outlay and extended timelines, setting the appropriate coupon rate is tantamount to balancing the cost of finance with market attractiveness. A project finance bond's coupon rate may articulate a premium, potentially elevated due to the risk profiles common in large-scale and infrastructural ventures (Esty, 2004). The rate offered takes into account factors such as the project's anticipated cash flows, the current interest rate environment, the underlying credit quality of the project or the issuing entity, and prevailing market rates for comparable risk instruments (Esty, 2004; Fabozzi, 2012).

The coupon frequency—or how often these interest payments are made to bondholders—is a variable factor, usually annual or semi-annual, depending on the norms of the market in which the bond is issued. Moreover, the coupon rate influences the bond's price sensitivity to interest rate changes; higher coupon bonds tend to be less affected by interest rate fluctuations when compared to lower coupon bonds, making them slightly less risky from a price volatility perspective (Fabozzi, 2012).

Understanding and strategically setting coupon rates are vital for successfully funding projects through the bond issuance route. For capital market professionals, the coupon rate signifies a benchmark for yield comparison across different securities. In contrast, project sponsors must comprehend that the set coupon rate, while it impacts investor appetite, simultaneously determines their regular interest payment obligations throughout the life of the bond. Insurance professionals, on the other hand, recognize the coupon payment obligations when assessing the risk profile and coverage terms for bond insurance products.

Coupon rates are an inseparable component of the bond structure that directly correlates to the cost of capital and the attractiveness of the bond issuance. As such, they require nuanced understanding and adept handling by finance professionals engaged in structuring, selling, and managing project finance bonds (Esty, 2004).

Maturity Dates As we dig deeper into the anatomy of a bond, understanding maturity dates is crucial for financiers and stakeholders involved in project finance. The maturity date of a bond is the exact date on which the principal amount of the bond, also referred to as the face value or par value, is scheduled to be paid back to the bondholder. This date signifies the culmination of the agreement between the issuer and the investor, marking the end of the bond's life, at which point the issuer's obligation to make regular interest payments ceases (Fabozzi, 2015).

Maturity dates can vary widely, from short-term bonds maturing in less than three years to long-term bonds with maturities extending beyond thirty years. These varying time frames cater to different investment strategies and the specific financing needs of a project. In the context of project finance, the maturity date is often aligned with the projected cash flow patterns of the financed project, ensuring that there will be sufficient revenue to meet the debt obligations (Yescombe, 2013).

The determination of an appropriate maturity date requires a careful analysis of the project's life cycle, anticipated revenues, and the economic environment. Project sponsors and others involved must perform rigorous due diligence to predict the timing and stability of cash flows, especially since these are the primary source of debt service in project finance. An improper alignment between cash flows and maturity dates can lead to liquidity issues, posing a serious risk to both parties (Esty, 2021).

From the perspective of the investor, the maturity date is a critical component of the bond's risk profile. Generally, longer maturities carry greater risk due to increased exposure to interest rate fluctuations, inflation, and the unpredictability of the distant future (Fabozzi, 2015). Therefore, understanding and negotiating maturity dates is an integral part of constructing an investment that matches the risk tolerance and time horizon of the investor.

It's imperative for professionals in banking, insurance, and capital markets to recognize the significance of maturity dates when structuring bonds for project finance. Careful consideration must be given to ensure that contract provisions regarding the maturity date align with the project's and investors' objectives. This alignment has a profound impact on the overall success of the financing structure, influencing the project's capacity to attract investment and achieve financial closure (Yescombe, 2013).

Face Values The face value of a bond, sometimes referred to as its par value or nominal value, is a critical concept in the architecture of bond financing. It represents the amount of money that the bond issuer promises to pay back to the bondholder at the maturity date (Fabozzi, 2018). Understanding how face value influences the financial dynamics of bonds is paramount for professionals operating in the project finance sector.

Initially, the issuer sets the face value and it often reflects a standard denomination prevalent in the market, providing a benchmark for investors when assessing and comparing bonds. Typically, bonds are issued with a face value of $1,000 in the U.S. market, though larger denominations are not uncommon for certain institutional transactions (Tuckman & Serrat, 2019).

The importance of face value extends beyond its representation as the repayment amount; it is also the basis for calculating interest payments, also known as coupons. These payments are a percentage of the bond's face value, so the total annual return to an investor is a function of this value and the coupon rate (Fabozzi, 2018). For example, a bond with a face value of $1,000 and a coupon rate of 5% will pay $50 in interest per year, typically in semi-annual instalments.

While the face value remains fixed until maturity, the bond's market value may fluctuate due to changes in market interest rates, credit quality of the issuer, and other macroeconomic factors. Professionals in the banking and insurance sectors, as well as those engaged in the capital markets, must be versed in these dynamics to guide their decision-making processes effectively. Understanding the relationship between face value, market value, and the coupon rate is essential in structuring deals that are attractive to both issuers and investors.

For project sponsors, determining an appropriate face value for bonds based on the scope and needs of the project is vital for ensuring the sufficiency of raised capital and the affordability of debt service. Incorporating the calculation of face values into financial models allows for scenario analysis, which aids in crafting a robust financial strategy under varying market conditions.

Ultimately, the role of face value in bond financing cannot be overstated. It influences investor perception, affects liquidity, and impacts the final cost of capital for the issuer. Mastery over this concept enables professionals to optimize financing structures that align with strategic investment goals and risk profiles. By bridging the gap between theory and practice, this foundational understanding contributes to the effective deployment of bonds as a vehicle for project finance.

The Lifecycle of Bonds

The lifecycle of a bond is a comprehensive journey that commences with the bond's issuance and culminates at its maturity or earlier redemption. To elucidate, this section will comparatively analyze each phase of a bond's existence from a market and project finance perspective.

The inception of the bond lifecycle transpires with its **issuance**, a process that involves intricate preparation, encompassing market research, formulation of a prospectus, and the necessary legal undertakings. During this embryonic stage, the terms of the bond—including coupon rates, maturity date, and face value—are steadfastly determined and communicated to potential investors (Fabozzi, 2018).

Following the issuance, the bond transitions into the **trading phase**. This stage is characterized by the secondary market activities where bonds are bought and sold among investors. The inherent value of the bond can fluctuate based on market conditions, interest rate movements, and the issuer's creditworthiness (Choudhry & Landuyt, 2018). Trading activities during this period largely dictate the yields received by bondholders and the cost of debt for the issuer.

The bond's maturity phase is a significant stage in the lifecycle when principal repayment is due. However, some bonds may offer **callable or puttable features**, enabling either the issuer or bondholder to accelerate the maturity of the bond under specified conditions (Hull, 2021). The implementation of such features can alter the anticipated lifecycle of the bond, providing flexibility to adapt to new financial circumstances or market conditions.

Projected finance bonds typically involve a strategic timeline for **coupon payments**. These can be structured as either fixed or variable payments, based on the terms set out at issuance, with the frequency and structure impacting the overall cash flow of the project being financed. The manner in which the interest obligations are met throughout the bond's lifecycle is crucial for maintaining the financial health of the project and the confidence of investors.

As bonds approach the twilight of their lifecycle, issuers must be mindful of **redemption strategies and refinancing options**. Particularly in the context of project finance, where long-term capital expenditures are involved, an issuer may seek to refinance the bonds an alternate to borrowing at potentially more favourable terms, reflecting changes in the entity's credit standing or shifts in interest rate environments (Fabozzi, 2018).

In some instances, an unforeseen eventuality may precipitate a bond's **early retirement** or default, triggering an entirely different set of actions, typically dictated by the terms articulated within the bond indenture. This can include seeking remedies, initiating restructuring efforts, or invoking the pertinent protective covenants designed to safeguard the interests of bondholders.

In concluding the lifecycle of a bond, understanding the sequence from issuance to maturity or redemption is imperative for stakeholders within the project finance domain. It enables better forecasting, enhances risk management strategies, and promotes informed decision-making consistent with the financial realities confronting a given project.

Chapter 4:
The Issuance Process

Pre-Issuance Considerations

The issuance of a bond is a complex process, which requires thorough preparation and a deep understanding of the market, regulatory requirements, and investor appetite. In the pre-issuance phase, project sponsors need to make strategic decisions about the structure and timing of the bond, the employment of legal and financial advisors, and the choice of underwriters. Each decision plays a critical role in the success of the bond issuance (Fabozzi, 2012).

Steps in Bond Issuance

The steps in the bond issuance process serve as a roadmap from initial planning to the final sale and distribution of the bonds. While this process can be broadly categorized into documentation, marketing, and pricing and sale, each phase requires meticulous attention to ensure regulatory compliance and market receptivity.

Documentation

Documentation is the foundation upon which a bond offering is built. This step involves the preparation of key legal documents, including the prospectus or offering statement, which provides detailed information about the bond issue and the project being financed. The issuer must also prepare resolutions and authorizations, along with other relevant disclosures, to provide transparency and fulfil legal obligations (Moody's Investors Service, 2020). Timely and accurate preparation of these documents is crucial as they are scrutinized by regulators, rating agencies, and potential investors.

Marketing

Effectively marketing the bond issue is essential to attract investment. During this phase, the issuer, along with their underwriter and financial advisors, will target investors that align with the bond's characteristics through roadshows, presentations, and one-on-one meetings. This stage is where the issuer's narrative around the bond's potential comes to the forefront, emphasizing the project's strengths and how the bond can meet investors' needs (Schwarcz, 2018).

Pricing and Sale

Pricing and sale mark the culmination of the issuance process. The bond's price is determined by myriad factors including market conditions, investor demand, and the financial health of the issuer. Following the pricing, the bonds are sold to investors, who will then provide the needed capital for the project. This step requires precise coordination and, often, quick decision-making to adapt to market dynamics (Fabozzi, 2012).

Post-Issuance Obligations

After the bonds have been issued, the issuer's responsibilities shift toward fulfilling ongoing obligations. These include regular financial reporting, adherence to covenants and agreements, and any other requirements set forth by the trust indenture or resolution. These post-issuance obligations are vital in maintaining investor confidence and ensuring compliance with regulatory standards (Securities and Exchange Commission, 2020).

Pre-Issuance Considerations

The terrain that lies before the issuance of bonds is both complex and exacting, requiring detailed navigation to mitigate risks and ensure compliance. Within the arena of project finance, pre-issuance considerations form the keystone holding together the arc of a successful bond offering. This begins with an exploration of the project's viability from both economic and regulatory perspectives.

Firstly, rigorous due diligence is paramount. One must delve into the financial projections, market analyses, and feasibility studies of the project at hand (Fabozzi, 2012). This investigation helps identify the underlying risks and the potential for sustainable cash flows to service debt obligations. The ability of the project to generate adequate revenue directly influences the structure of the bond and the confidence of prospective investors.

Concurrent to financial scrutiny, legal due diligence is equally critical. The engagement of competent legal counsel ensures that all regulatory requirements are met and that the proposed bond issuance conforms to jurisdictional statutes. Local and international regulations may either impede or facilitate certain bond structures; thus, an intimate understanding of these frameworks is indispensable (Securities and Exchange Commission, 2020).

Another critical factor is the credit assessment. Credit ratings, allocated by reputable agencies, imbue investors with a metric of trust. The rating exercise determines the project's credit risk and influences interest costs; therefore, engaging with credit rating agencies early in the process is a judicious step (Moody's Investor's Service, 2019).

Strategic decisions regarding the type and terms of the bond are vital as well. Decisions regarding whether the bonds issued should be fixed or variable rate, or the maturity length that will align with the projected income stream of the project, must be meticulously calibrated (Fabozzi, 2012). Additionally, considerations related to secured versus unsecured bonds, or senior versus subordinate debt, can have lasting implications on the cost and appeal of the bond offering.

Lastly, project sponsors must weigh the market environment. The interest rate climate, market liquidity, and investor appetite all dictate the timing and scale of bond issuance. The integration of environmental, social, and governance (ESG) criteria into bond offerings is also becoming progressively important, providing an impetus for projects that demonstrate a commitment to broader societal and environmental objectives.

In summary, before embarking upon the issuance process, it's crucial that project sponsors, along with their banking and legal partners, methodically address the multifaceted elements enumerated above. Failure to allocate the necessary resources and attention to pre-issuance considerations can jeopardize the entire endeavour, emphasizing the saliency of this preparatory phase in the issuance process.

Steps in Bond Issuance

The issuance of bonds is a complex and strategic process that enables project sponsors to raise large amounts of funding from the capital markets. It is essential for those involved to understand each step meticulously to ensure a smooth transaction that aligns with regulatory requirements and market expectations. The stages of bond issuance follow a general pattern though specifics may vary depending on bond type, jurisdiction, and other factors.

1. **Appointing the Advisory Team:** Initially, the issuer must assemble a proficient team, including investment bankers, legal counsel, and financial advisors (Kraemer et al., 2013). These professionals offer the expertise needed across various aspects

of the transaction, from structuring the bond to ensuring compliance with regulatory standards.

2. **Preparation of Legal Documentation:** Preparing the necessary legal documents is one of the most crucial steps in the bond issuance process. This involves drafting the prospectus or official statement, which contains all relevant details about the issuer, the project being financed, and the terms of the bond (Fabozzi, 2012).

3. **Credit Rating:** Obtaining a credit rating is a step that can significantly influence investor perception and the bond's pricing. The rating provided by agencies like Moody's or Standard & Poor's reflects the issuer's ability to repay the debt (Standard & Poor's Financial Services LLC, 2021).

4. **Marketing:** The issuer and underwriters market the bond to potential investors through presentations, meetings, and roadshows. They must provide comprehensive details about the bond offering to enable investors to make informed decisions.

5. **Pricing the Bond:** Pricing the bond involves determining the interest rate and price at which the bonds will be sold. Various factors, including current market conditions, the issuer's credit worthiness, and investor demand, contribute to the bond's pricing (Fabozzi, 2012).

6. **Sale and Distribution:** The bonds are then sold to investors either through a public offering or a private placement. The underwriters play a crucial role in this process, helping to ensure the bonds are distributed effectively and efficiently.

7. **Settlement and Issuance:** On the settlement date, investors pay for the purchased bonds, and the issuer receives the funds. At this point, the bonds are issued, and the issuer becomes

obligated to make interest payments and return the principal upon maturity.

8. **Closing the Transaction:** The final step involves the completion of all legal and operational tasks related to the bond issuance, which includes reporting and closing entries in the accounting records of the issuer (Fabozzi, 2012).

Bond issuance is a critical area of project finance that requires careful planning and execution. Each step comes with its own set of considerations and requires coordinated efforts from various parties involved in the transaction. Understandably, this structured approach needs to be tailored to meet specific project needs while adhering to market and regulatory norms.

Documentation in the context of bond issuance stands as a crucial element, embodying the legal and transactional framework that underpins the relationship between the issuer, the investors, and other stakeholders. Effective documentation ensures clarity in the terms of the bond, secures the legal enforceability of the contractual obligations, and serves to communicate vital information to investors thereby supporting the credibility of the issue (Schwarcz, 2002).

The primary documents include the indenture or trust deed, which is a contract between the issuer and the bondholders, usually represented by a trustee. This document stipulates the binding terms, rights, and duties of the involved parties throughout the lifecycle of the bond and includes vital details such as the interest rate, maturity date, collateral arrangements, and covenants. Furthermore, the official statement or prospectus provides a detailed disclosure of the bond offering, including the issuer's financial position, details of the project, use of proceeds, and specific risk factors associated with the bond offering (Hill et al., 2010).

Legal counsel plays a pivotal role in documenting a bond issuance. They ensure compliance with the relevant securities laws and regulations, and that the documents are accurately drafted to mitigate potential legal disputes. The offering document, a legal and binding agreement, must be scrupulously reviewed by potential investors who rely on its contents for making informed decisions regarding their investments (Miller, 2011).

Critical to this process is the due diligence undertaken to ensure the accuracy of the information contained within the offering documents. Parties involved in the documentation process, particularly the underwriters and legal advisors, must conduct a thorough investigation into the financial health and prospects of the issuer and the viability of the project being financed (Miller, 2011).

In summary, documentation in bond issuance is not just about fulfilling a regulatory requirement; it fundamentally weaves the relationship of trust and understanding among parties, and ensures the bond market's integrity and functionality.

Marketing Within the broad ambit of bond issuance, marketing emerges as a pivotal phase, constituting the bridge between preparation and execution for project sponsors and capital market professionals. The core objective of the marketing phase is to foster interest and underscoring the value proposition of the bond issue to potential investors. Key to this process is the development of a comprehensive marketing strategy, tailored to elucidate the unique aspects of the project being financed—positioning it as an attractive investment opportunity.

Marketing begins with the crafting of the investment story, a narrative that encapsulates the strengths, opportunities, the underlying project's economic rationale, and its alignment with broader market trends (Fabozzi et al., 2012). Elaborating on critical financial metrics and projections can signify security and potential yield, resonating with the investors' quests for reliable returns. Identifying the target investor demographic is also crucial—from institutional investors with a focus on long-term, stable returns to retail investors attracted to specific project aspects such as sustainability or community impact.

A multidisciplinary team, often led by the underwriters, spearheads the promotion of the bond issuance. By deploying a mix of traditional and digital communication tools such as investment memorandums, presentations, roadshows, and web-based platforms, they can amplify reach and deepen investor engagement. Roadshows, in particular, serve as a conduit for direct interaction between issuers and potential investors, facilitating a deeper comprehension of the project details, issuer's credibility, and the associated risks (Kidwell et al., 2016).

Digital platforms and social media presence can augment traditional outreach efforts. Virtual roadshows and webinars can broaden the audience and make the proposition accessible to a global investor pool (Kidwell et al., 2016). Ultimately, the aggregated impact of these marketing endeavours hinges on their ability to reach a tailored set of investors and convincingly address their risk-return profiles.

Throughout this marketing phase, transparency is paramount. Clear disclosure of potential risks alongside opportunities must align with the legal and regulatory frameworks governing bond issuances. This balanced approach not only ensures compliance but also engenders trust and credibility among potential investors—who are essential for the successful placement of a bond issue.

Pricing and Sale Within the sphere of bond issuance for project finance, the 'Pricing and Sale' stage represents a critical juncture that determines the cost of capital for the project sponsor and the potential yield for investors. It involves setting the price and interest rates of the bonds in a manner that reflects the underlying project's risk profile while ensuring sufficient demand in the capital markets.

For bankers, project sponsors, and insurance professionals alike, understanding this phase is paramount, as it directly impacts the financial viability and success of the financing endeavour. The pricing mechanism typically hinges on several factors, including market conditions, the creditworthiness of the issuer, and prevailing interest rates. It can involve complex modelling to project the future cash flows of the project being financed and determine the appropriate yield for investors that compensates for the risks involved (Fabozzi, 2015).

In practice, the pricing process is generally conducted by the underwriters, who formulate a preliminary price range through pre-marketing activities. This often involves conducting a yield analysis, which seeks to compare the bond's proposed interest rates with those of existing securities with similar credit profiles (Brigham & Ehrhardt, 2016). Underwriters and project sponsors must work collaboratively during this phase as pricing inefficiencies can result in the bond being under- or oversubscribed.

The actual sale of the bonds is executed through either public offerings or private placements. In public offerings, bonds are made available to a broad investor base, which may include retail and institutional investors. Conversely, private placements are restricted to a limited number of sophisticated investors. The chosen method has implications for both regulatory compliance and the depth of demand that can be accessed (Fabozzi, 2015).

Ultimately, it is the interplay between the coupon rate, the project's risk profile, market appetite, and timing that dictates the success of this stage. Ensuring that the bonds are favourably priced to sell in full but without leaving money on the table requires a nuanced understanding of financial markets and is indeed an artful balance.

The outcome of the pricing and sale phase must be weighed against the project's financial targets, with a keen awareness of how divergences can affect the overall cost of financing. Professionals in the field must be aware of the dynamic nature of capital markets and be prepared to adapt strategies in real-time to ensure the bonds are sold at the optimal price, thus laying a robust financial foundation for the project's future (Harrison, 2013).

Post-Issuance Obligations

Once bonds have been successfully issued, the issuer's responsibilities transition from the issuance process to ongoing obligations. Primarily, these obligations ensure that the issuer remains in compliance with both regulatory requirements and covenants established in the issuance documentation. It can't be overstated how crucial these post-issuance obligations are; they ensure that the trust placed in the issuer by the investors is upheld and that the legal and financial integrity of the issuance remains intact over the bond's lifecycle.

To begin with, the issuer must adhere to any continuing disclosure agreements that are part of the bond documentation. These disclosures often require periodic updates on the issuer's financial health, project progress, or any other information deemed material to the bond's value or the issuer's ability to repay the bond. A failure to provide the ongoing disclosure can lead to regulatory penalties and a loss of investor confidence, which can impact the issuer's credit rating and ability to raise funds in the future (Securities and Exchange Commission [SEC], 2020).

The issuer also has a duty to ensure timely payment of coupon rates to bondholders. This obligation pertains to both interest payments and the repayment of principal upon maturity. Late or missed payments could lead to events of default, with severe consequences including potential acceleration of debt repayment, legal action, or negative impacts on the issuer's market reputation and credit standing (Mooradian & Wachowicz, 2016).

Additionally, issuers may have to comply with various covenants, either affirmative, requiring certain actions, or negative, prohibiting certain activities. For instance, debt covenants may restrict the issuer's ability to take on additional debt or sell significant assets without creditor approval. Maintaining compliance with these covenants is a critical aspect of post-issuance obligations, as a covenant breach can also lead to default (Smith & Warner, 1979).

Another post-issuance responsibility involves tax compliance. For tax-exempt bonds, issuers must ensure that the projects financed by the bonds meet the requirements set forth under tax statutes and regulations. Failure to comply can result in the bonds becoming retroactively taxable, which may have significant financial repercussions for bondholders and the issuer alike.

Monitoring and meeting post-issuance obligations is not a task to approach passively. Issuers often employ trustees, paying agents, and compliance professionals to oversee and certify that all requirements are being met throughout the life of the bond. These parties play instrumental roles in protecting the interests of bondholders and assisting the issuer in upholding their fiduciary duties.

Overall, diligent management of post-issuance obligations is an integral component of the trust structure built between issuers, investors, and regulators. It is the linchpin holding together the long-term viability and success of a bond issuance, securing a sustainable financial foundation for project development and other capital needs. Following these guidelines not only promotes transparency and accountability but also positions the issuer favourably for future capital market engagements.

Chapter 5:
Players in the Bond Issuance Ecosystem

The seamless operation of the bond issuance process is contingent upon the coordinated efforts of multiple participants, each with a specialized role. Understanding the players in the bond issuance ecosystem is critical for bankers, project sponsors, insurance professionals, and capital market experts looking to navigate the intricacies of financing projects through bonds.

Issuers

At the heart of the bond market are the issuers: these can be corporations, municipalities, or governments that need to raise capital for various purposes, including financing large projects. The issuer is responsible for defining the bond's terms, including the coupon rate, maturity, and covenants, and is ultimately liable for making timely interest payments and returning the principal to bondholders. Navigating through the complex process of issuing bonds requires thorough knowledge of market conditions and investor expectations, often necessitating expert advisory services (Fabozzi, 2018).

Underwriters

Underwriters, typically investment banks, play a vital role in the bond issuance process. They evaluate the risks associated with the bond issuance, advise on the pricing and structure of the bond, and undertake the critical function of purchasing securities from the issuer and selling them to investors, ensuring that the issuer secures the needed capital (Smith & Smith, 2020).

Legal Counsel and Advisors

Legal counsel and advisors ensure all regulatory requirements are met and the issuance complies with applicable laws. They draft the official statement or prospectus, which provides detailed information on the bond offering, and assist with the structuring of the transaction, protecting the issuer's and investors' interests through the enforcement of covenants and terms (Henderson et al., 2021).

Trustee and Paying Agents

Trustees oversee the issuer's compliance with the covenants and terms agreed upon in the bond indenture. They act on behalf of bondholders to enforce rights if the issuer defaults. Paying agents handle the administrative side, processing interest and principal payments to bondholders. The trustee often assumes the role of the paying agent as part of their duties, providing a critical link between the issuer and the bondholders (Fabozzi, 2018).

The synergy among these participants drives the efficiency of the bond issuance process. Each entity is a cog in the well-oiled machine that translates capital needs into effective funding tools, ensuring the market operates smoothly. As these roles are deeply interwoven, the success of a bond issuance relies heavily on the expertise and collaboration of each player within the ecosystem.

Issuers

The term 'issuer' refers to the entities that originate bonds as a means to raise capital. Issuers are the bedrock of the bond issuance ecosystem, leveraging debt as a tool for financing a vast array of endeavours—from government infrastructure projects to corporate expansion efforts.

Within this sphere, a variety of issuers come to the fore, each with distinct objectives and regulatory frameworks guiding their actions.

Firstly, sovereign governments frequently issue bonds to fund budgetary needs, infrastructure projects, and public services. Similarly, sub-sovereign entities, such as states, provinces, and municipalities, issue debt to finance local initiatives (Fabozzi, 2018). These are often seen in the form of municipal bonds, which can be further categorized into general obligation bonds and revenue bonds, and they're typically subject to tax considerations different from corporate bonds.

Corporations also constitute a significant segment of bond issuers. Corporate bonds are utilized to raise capital for a range of reasons, such as business expansion, acquisition financing, or capital restructuring. The intricacies of corporate bond issuances often call for elaborate planning and negotiation, involving a detailed examination of the corporate's financial status, creditworthiness, and the intended use of proceeds.

Financial institutions are another principal issuer, utilizing bonds to manage their long-term funding and regulatory capital requirements. Meanwhile, project sponsors may issue project bonds specifically tied to the cash flows of a commercial project, exemplifying a focused deployment of bonds within a structured finance environment.

Beyond these traditional actors, quasi-governmental organizations, supranational bodies, and non-profit organizations also emerge as issuers in the global bond market. Notably, in recent times, there's been an uptick in the issuance of environmental, social, and governance (ESG) bonds by a range of issuers, addressing investors' growing appetite for sustainable investment opportunities.

A fundamental aspect of an issuer's role is understanding the associated obligations and adhering to stringent regulatory and compliance measures post-issuance. Issuers must maintain a consistent stream of communication with underwriters, investors, and rating agencies, manage their credit profile, and navigate repayment and refinancing options efficiently to minimize the cost of borrowing (Moody's Investors Service, 2020).

Understanding the distinctive roles and responsibilities of issuers is vital for the capital markets community. Without a thorough grasp of the nuances associated with different issuers, professionals might not achieve the sophisticated insight necessary for optimizing financial structures or providing adequate advice on managing the myriad risk factors inherent to bond issuances.

Underwriters

In the bond issuance ecosystem, underwriters play a pivotal role in originating, structuring, and executing the sale of bonds to finance various types of projects. Typically, investment banks or specialized underwriting firms serve as the underwriters who undertake a comprehensive due diligence process to ensure the success of a bond offering (Fabozzi & Mann, 2020). Their primary responsibilities include advising the issuer on the timing of the sale, determining the bond's initial price, formulating the offering structure, and managing the distribution of the bonds to investors.

In a process known as underwriting, these financial intermediaries commit to purchasing the entire issue of bonds from the issuer and then resell them to the public and institutional investors (Amihud, Mendelson, & Pedersen, 2019). This commitment provides the issuer with the assurance of receiving the capital needed and transfers the risk of inadequate demand from the issuer to the underwriter. Furthermore, underwriters employ their market expertise to aid issuers in navigating the complexities of regulatory compliance and market dynamics, helping to optimize the bond terms to attract investors while remaining in line with the issuer's financing objectives.

Underwriters also conduct risk assessment and engage in the pricing of the bond issuance. The risk assessment involves analyzing the credit quality of the issuer, economic conditions, and the project's specifics to set a yield that reflects the perceived risk associated with the bond. Subsequently, they provide the issuer with a suggested interest rate or coupon that balances investor demand with the cost of borrowing for the issuer.

Marketing, a critical phase managed by underwriters, ensures the bonds reach the target audience. They often organize roadshows and presentations to promote the issuance to potential investors, providing insights into the creditworthiness of the issuer and the project financed by the bond (Fabozzi & Mann, 2020). Additionally, underwriters are instrumental in creating the offering memorandum—a key document that describes the bond's features, risks, and the terms of the offering.

Once the issuance is ready to proceed, underwriters lead the book-building process, during which they collect indications of interest from potential investors to gauge the demand for the bonds. This process influences the final pricing and allocation of the bonds, with the aim being to maximize the issuer's interests and ensure a successful sell-out of the bond issue.

The final act of underwriters in the bond issuance process involves stabilization. They may buy bonds in the secondary market post-issuance to prevent or mitigate price volatility. Such actions are governed by specific regulatory provisions to ensure market transparency and fairness (Choudhry, 2020).

Overall, the underwriters' expertise in financial markets and distribution networks is crucial for determining the appropriate structure, price, and placement of the bonds, with substantial repercussions for the issuer's cost of capital and overall success of the bond issuance.

Legal Counsel and Advisors

Legal counsel and advisors play an instrumental role in the bond issuance ecosystem. Within the sphere of project finance, these professionals ensure that issuances comply with the relevant legal and regulatory frameworks, advise on structuring dealings to be favourable to their clients while being compliant, and facilitate smooth transactions.

Legal experts such as bond counsel, disclosure counsel, and tax attorneys provide counsel on a variety of matters. They prepare the necessary documents which may include the bond indenture, resolutions, opinions, and ensure they contain protective covenants for bondholders. They also deal with any legal hurdles that may arise in the complex transactional environment of bond issuance.

Navigating the intricate landscape of securities laws, they work hand-in-hand with issuers to prepare official statements and prospectuses that accurately describe the bond offering to investors (Securities Act of 1933; Trust Indenture Act of 1939). Moreover, their involvement is crucial when it comes to continuing disclosure compliance under the Securities Exchange Act of 1934 and meeting the stipulations laid down by regulatory bodies such as the Securities and Exchange Commission (SEC).

Tax attorneys ensure that, where applicable, the bond issuance takes advantage of tax-exempt status, saving costs for the issuer and providing potential tax benefits to bondholders. They meticulously plan out the tax implications of the bond terms, considering both current tax laws and any foreseeable changes that could impact the project's financials (Kleinbard et al., 2017).

Furthermore, advisors ascertain the due diligence is properly conducted, protecting all involved parties from future disputes or financial mishaps. They play a part in risk mitigation by identifying legal risks and advising on necessary risk management strategies, interfacing with trustees, and guiding issuers on compliance with legal obligations post-issuance. Additionally, they may assist in executing agreements with underwriters and trustees and in negotiations with potential investors.

Given their role in ensuring that bond issuances are executed within the bounds of the law and that financial disclosures are made transparently and accurately, legal counsel and advisors contribute to the integrity and efficiency of the market (Frankel et al., 2016). Their expertise is not just crucial for navigating current frameworks but also for adapting to legal transformations that may occur over the life of a bond, as they are pivotal in handling any legal amendments or restructurings needed.

In sum, legal counsel and advisors are indispensable stewards of legal compliance and strategic planning in the project finance bond issuance process. Their guidance is critical in the formation, maintenance, and successful conclusion of bond offerings. As such, they hold a respected and necessary position within the bond issuance ecosystem.

Trustee and Paying Agents

Within the bond issuance ecosystem, trustees and paying agents perform critical roles that are central to the administration and success of bond financing for projects. A trustee, usually a bank or a financial institution with fiduciary powers, is appointed to act on behalf of the bondholders to ensure that the issuer complies with the terms of the bond indenture, which is the legal document outlining the obligations and rights of all parties involved in the bond transaction (Fabozzi, 2016).

The trustee's responsibilities include monitoring the issuer's compliance with covenants, managing the flow of interest and principal payments from the issuer to the bondholders, and in cases of default, representing the bondholders' interests in legal proceedings. The trustee provides an assurance to the bondholders that an independent entity is overseeing the issuer's adherence to the bond terms. This role is particularly important in project finance where large sums are financed and the projects often involve a range of stakeholders with complex agreements in place.

On the other hand, a paying agent is appointed by the issuer to manage the actual disbursement of funds to bondholders. They typically handle the administration involved in processing interest payments and the repayment of principal at maturity or upon early redemption. The paying agency agreement, which supplements the bond indenture, specifies the duties of the paying agent which include accepting funds from the issuer, maintaining payment records, and distributing payments accurately and promptly to bondholders (Moody's Investors Service, 2017).

Both trustees and paying agents serve to reduce the potential for conflicts of interest between the issuer and the bondholders. Their involvement is meant to provide transparency and a level playing field in transactions, which can be crucial in maintaining investor confidence, especially in the high-stakes environment of project financing (Standard & Poor's Financial Services LLC, 2018). By ensuring that the issuer's obligation to the bondholders is enforced and that interest and principal payments are processed efficiently, trustees and paying agents solidify the trust and functional performance necessary for the fluid operation of the bond market.

Chapter 6:
Rating Agencies and Their Significance

Rating agencies are pivotal in the arena of bond issuances, as they provide a critical assessment of the creditworthiness of bond issuers which includes governments, municipalities, companies, and structured finance instruments. The importance of rating agencies lies mainly in their ability to influence the yield required by investors and the level of interest rates that issuers must offer in order to attract investment.

The Credit Rating Process

The credit rating process begins with an analysis of the issuer's financial statements, examining revenue streams, expenses, existing debt, and cash flow patterns. Rating agencies also evaluate sector risks, regulatory landscape, and macroeconomic variables that could affect the issuer's ability to meet its debt obligations (White, 2010). Each of these factors is factored into a rating model that yields a rating symbol indicating the level of risk associated with the bond. These ratings range from 'AAA' for the highest credit quality to 'D' for issuers that are already in default. Moody's, Standard & Poor's, and Fitch Ratings are the three foremost agencies in this domain, each with their own set of rating criteria and scales.

How Ratings Impact Bond Issuance

Bond ratings directly influence the cost of capital for issuers and the investment decisions of investors. A higher rating typically results in lower interest rates, reducing the issuer's cost of borrowing. Conversely, a lower rating signifies higher risk, which requires higher yields to compensate investors for that risk (Fabozzi et al., 2012). Rating changes, either upgrades or downgrades, can also affect the price of bonds already in circulation, directly impacting the market value of those bonds.

Navigating Credit Enhancement Strategies

To potentially obtain better credit ratings or to make bond issues more attractive, issuers may employ various credit enhancement strategies. These might include the procurement of bond insurance, the use of surety bonds, or the establishment of reserve funds (Schwarcz, 2002). Other enhancements involve structuring the bond as secured debt, providing collateral, or guaranteeing the debt with corporate or governmental guarantees. Such credit enhancements are tailored to mitigate the perceived risks by rating agencies and investors, often resulting in improved ratings and a broader investor base for the bond issue.

The Credit Rating Process

Understanding the credit rating process is indispensable for players across the financing spectrum, from bankers to capital market professionals. Credit ratings play a pivotal role in determining the cost and availability of capital for project sponsors. These ratings, produced by agencies such as Moody's, Standard & Poor's, and Fitch, are essential in assessing the creditworthiness of debt issuers and the financial instruments they offer.

The process begins with the issuer's request for a rating from a credit rating agency, initiating a thorough analysis of the issuer's financial condition, which includes an examination of financial statements, management quality, asset base, and existing debt obligations (White, 2018). Additionally, the agency reviews external market conditions, industry trends, and regulatory environments that may affect the issuer's ability to meet debt obligations.

Rating agencies then employ their proprietary methodologies to assess default risk, which results in a rating that mirrors the agency's opinion on the issuer's creditworthiness. The underlying components of this evaluation include quantitative factors, such as debt service coverage ratios and interest coverage ratios, alongside qualitative factors, like corporate strategy and risk management practices (Langohr & Langohr, 2008).

The outcome of this process is a credit rating, which typically ranges from 'AAA' for the highest quality bonds, reflecting the lowest level of credit risk, down to 'C' or 'D', indicating high risk or default. These ratings are not only pivotal for investors but also influence the terms at which issuers can raise debt, with higher ratings generally resulting in lower interest rates (Cantor & Packer, 1996).

Once assigned, ratings are not static. Continuous surveillance by the credit rating agency is required to identify any material changes in the issuer's financial health. If such changes occur, the agency can revise the credit rating accordingly to reflect the new risk level. This monitoring ensures that the current rating always reflects the latest view of the creditworthiness of the issuer.

It is imperative for banking and finance professionals to comprehend the nuances of credit ratings as these evaluations provide insights into the risk profile of bond issuances. A deep understanding of the critics and methodologies employed in the credit rating process empowers professionals to make more informed decisions regarding project finance and bond investments.

How Ratings Impact Bond Issuance

The facilitation of bond issuance is significantly influenced by credit ratings ascribed by esteemed rating agencies. These ratings are reflective metrics of the issuer's creditworthiness and the associated risks concerning timely payment of interest and principal on the bond. Bond issuances, embedded within the sphere of project finance, carry heightened attention to these ratings due to the intricate risk assessments they encapsulate (Fabozzi, 2018).

At the onset, credit ratings affect a bond's appeal to investors. High ratings, typically ranging from AAA to AA by Standard & Poor's or Aaa to Aa by Moody's, signal lower credit risk, thereby attracting a broader pool of investors. Contrastingly, bonds with lower ratings may have to offer higher interest rates to compensate investors for the increased risk that these ratings imply (Kidwell et al., 2016).

The convergence of a bond's yield and its rating is evident. High-grade ratings can facilitate lower borrowing costs for issuers due to the implied safety; conversely, lower-grade ratings necessitate higher yields to lure investors. This risk-return trade-off is crucial in determining the funding cost of a project (Fabozzi, 2018). In essence, the cost of capital for a project is intrinsically linked to the bond's assigned rating.

Furthermore, ratings impact the structuring strategy of the issuance. For instance, a suboptimal rating may prompt the issuer to incorporate credit enhancement mechanisms such as sureties, guarantees, or letters of credit to augment the bond's appeal. Such enhancements, while potentially elevating the cost, might be indispensable in achieving a successful issuance (Kidwell et al., 2016).

Credit rating agencies also engage in surveillance post-issuance, offering upgrades or downgrades based on fiscal discipline, market conditions, and agency evaluation. The existence of dynamic rating actions necessitates issuers to adhere to prudent financial management to maintain or improve ratings over time, which in turn affects the marketability and refinancing opportunities for the bond.

In sum, credit ratings hold immense sway over the nature and success of bond issuances in project finance. These ratings serve as a linchpin in the decision-making process for investors and issuers alike, shaping the financial landscape of a project from inception to maturity. Hence, comprehension of the profound implications borne by these ratings constitutes an essential facet of capital market expertise.

Navigating Credit Enhancement Strategies

In project finance, securing an investment-grade credit rating is crucial for issuers to attract institutional investors and decrease the cost of capital. Rating agencies such as Standard & Poor's, Moody's, and Fitch play a pivotal role in the evaluation of bonds, but their ratings are not static. Issuers can proactively influence their credit ratings through credit enhancement strategies that lower the risk profile of their bond offerings (Fabozzi & Kothari, 2008).

Credit enhancement, in essence, involves the use of mechanisms or instruments to raise the credit profile of the debt issue. These enhancements can be internal or external to the bond structure. Internal enhancements include reserve funds, over-collateralization, and subordinate tranches that create a cushion for senior bondholders against defaults. External enhancements might involve guarantees, letters of credit provided by third parties, or bond insurance. Such enhancements are particularly noteworthy as they provide an additional layer of security, assuring bond investors that their investment is safeguarded against default (Smith & Walter, 2002).

One of the most common forms of credit enhancement is bond insurance, where an insurance company commits to pay interest and principal payments should the issuer default. The insurer's creditworthiness effectively substitutes for the issuer's, thereby enabling the bond to achieve a higher rating (Monk & Wagner, 2012). It's important for participants such as bankers and project sponsors to evaluate the cost of these enhancements against the potential reduction in interest costs achieved by improving the bond's rating. Any credit improvement comes at a cost, and the decision to apply these enhancements must be grounded in a meticulous financial analysis that weighs expected benefits against additional expenses.

Another consideration is the structure of the credit enhancement itself. Standby letters of credit (SLOCs) provided by banks are contracts where the bank ensures payment on behalf of the bond issuer if they cannot meet their obligations. While SLOCs provide a high level of security, they can be costly and typically are used for shorter-term maturities. For project finance deals that span decades, establishing a sinking fund or using wrap insurance, which ensures the entirety of the bond issue, might be more appropriate (Fabozzi & Kothari, 2008).

In summary, navigating credit enhancement strategies is integral to bond issuance within project finance. These strategies can lower the perceived risk of default, which in turn can lead to more favourable credit ratings and reduced costs of borrowing. However, the implementation of these credit enhancements comes at a cost, which issuers must carefully evaluate against the expected benefits. By understanding the various tools available for credit enhancement and their appropriate contexts, financial professionals can adeptly manoeuvre the challenges of securing favourable interest rates and investment terms in their bond offerings.

Chapter 7:
Understanding Risk in Bond Financing

O ne of the pivotal considerations in bond financing is the assessment and management of risks. Bond issuances, whether aimed at funding infrastructure projects or corporate expansion, entail a multitude of inherent risks that can significantly influence the cost and viability of a project. This chapter seeks to elucidate the primary risks associated with bond financing, namely market risk, credit risk, liquidity risk, as well as legal and regulatory risks. Understanding these risks empowers stakeholders to make informed decisions and effectively tailor their risk mitigation strategies.

Market Risk

Market risk refers to the potential for investment losses due to factors that affect the entire trading market. Bond markets, like others, are subject to forces such as changes in interest rates, economic downturns, and shifts in investor sentiment which can affect bond prices and yields. A rise in interest rates generally results in a decline in bond prices, adversely affecting fixed-income securities. Project sponsors and investors need a keen understanding of the interest rate environment and its influencing economic indicators to anticipate such changes effectively (Fabozzi, 2018).

Credit Risk

Credit risk, or default risk, concerns the possibility that the bond issuer will be unable to meet principal or interest payments. It reflects the issuer's financial position and the project's earning capacity and affects bond valuation and the perceived quality of the bond issue. The riskier an investment is deemed, the higher the yield investors will demand to compensate for this risk. Credit Ratings provided by rating agencies are a common measure used to assess and communicate the credit risk of different bond issuances (Moody's Investor Services, 2021).

Liquidity Risk

Liquidity risk relates to the ease with which a bond can be bought or sold without impacting its market price. High liquidity means that there are sufficient buyers and sellers at any given time. On the other hand, a bond with low liquidity might not be easily marketable without accepting a discount on the price, which can be particularly disadvantageous for investors needing to liquidate their holdings promptly. Factors influencing a bond's liquidity include its market demand, credit quality, and time to maturity (Amihud et al., 2005).

Legal and Regulatory Risks

Legal and regulatory risks encompass the potential for losses due to changes in laws, regulations, or court rulings. This is a critical consideration in bond financing, as compliance with regulatory requirements is mandatory for issuance and ongoing operations. Bond issuers must stay abreast of changes in securities laws, environmental regulations, and any regulation that could affect the bond's terms, tax status, or the project's viability (Kane, 1981).

Effective risk management involves identifying, evaluating, and implementing strategies to mitigate these risks. Diversification, credit enhancement, duration management, and staying informed on legal and regulatory changes are some tactics employed to manage these risks. The ultimate goal is to ensure the bond's attractiveness to investors, maintain financial stability for the issuer, and contribute to the project's success.

Market Risk

Market risk, also known as systematic risk, refers to the possibility of an investment losing value due to the factors that affect the overall performance of the financial markets. In the context of bond financing, market risk encompasses several variables that can adversely impact the value and yield of bonds. These factors include changes in interest rates, inflation rates, and general economic conditions (Tuckman & Serrat, 2011).

Interest rate risk is a primary concern in bond financing. It arises when there is a fluctuation in the prevailing interest rates in the economy that is inversely related to the bond prices. When interest rates increase, the value of existing bonds typically decreases to adjust the fixed income from bonds to the more attractive current market rates (Fabozzi, 2018). For project sponsors, this means a potential decline in the market value of the bonds they have issued, which can become significantly relevant if they need to repurchase or retire debt before maturity.

Inflation risk is another critical aspect of market risk. It refers to the erosion of the purchasing power of the bond's future cash flows due to an increase in prices for goods and services, which can erode the real return on bonds. Inflation can diminish the purchasing power of fixed-interest payments from bonds, making them less attractive to investors aiming for a certain real return target (Brigham & Ehrhardt, 2013).

Apart from interest rate and inflation risks, economic conditions can have a profound effect on bond financing. Economic downturns, geopolitical events, or significant policy shifts can result in changes to the demand and supply dynamics for bonds, affecting their pricing and liquidity in the market. Therefore, understanding and managing market risk is critical for all participants in bond financing.

Considering the potential impact of market risk on bond investments, it is fundamental for those involved in bond issuance and trading—like bankers, project sponsors, insurance professionals, and capital market professionals—to employ strategies to mitigate these risks. These strategies can include diversification, asset-liability matching, and the use of derivatives such as interest rate swaps and futures contracts to hedge against market volatility (Fabozzi, 2018).

In summary, market risk plays an essential role in bond financing and necessitates careful analysis by professionals involved in the issuance and management of bond investments. Awareness and proactive management of market risk can aid in maintaining the financial stability and attractiveness of bond issues as a viable financing tool for projects.

Credit Risk

In the context of bond financing, credit risk refers to the possibility that a borrower will default on their debt obligations, leading to financial loss for the lender or investor. This risk is particularly pertinent in the realm of bond financing where the issuers of bonds, be they corporations, municipalities, or other entities, might face circumstances that impede their ability to make timely payments of interest or principal. Understanding and managing credit risk is crucial for investors, as it can significantly affect the yield and value of a bond investment (Fabozzi, 2012).

Credit risk in bond financing is inherently tied to the creditworthiness of the issuer. Credit rating agencies, such as Standard & Poor's, Moody's, and Fitch Ratings, play a fundamental role in assessing an issuer's financial health. They analyze a range of factors including the issuer's financial statements, debt levels, operating performance, and any potential legal or environmental liabilities. Based on these evaluations, they assign credit ratings that serve as a shorthand indicator of credit risk (Mooradian & Burkhardt, 1996). Bond issuers with higher credit ratings are perceived as less risky, and thus generally pay lower interest rates compared to those with lower credit ratings.

The process by which credit risk is assessed includes both quantitative and qualitative analysis. Quantitative analysis involves examining financial metrics such as debt-to-equity ratios, interest coverage ratios, and cash flow stability. Qualitative analysis, on the other hand, looks at factors such as management expertise, industry position, and regulatory environment (Altman, 1968). Together, these assessments form a comprehensive view of an issuer's credit risk profile.

Mitigation strategies for credit risk in bond financing include the use of credit enhancements, such as guarantees, letters of credit, or bond insurance. These instruments can improve the credit profile of an issue and attract a wider investor base by providing additional security to the bondholders. In addition, investors can manage credit risk by diversifying their bond portfolios across different issuers, industries, and geographies.

Understanding credit risk is not only essential for the initial investment decision but also for ongoing monitoring. The financial condition of an issuer can change over time due to a variety of factors, making it imperative for investors to remain vigilant and responsive to new information and market developments which can influence the issuer's ability to meet its obligations.

Liquidity Risk

Liquidity risk in bond financing refers to the possibility that a bond may not be readily saleable on the secondary market without a substantial change in price and may consequently impact an investor's or issuer's ability to execute transactions promptly and efficiently. This kind of risk is particularly pertinent to bonds issued for project financing, where the specificity of the project or the lack of a broad investor base can lead to reduced marketability (Fabozzi et al., 2014).

When evaluating liquidity risk, it's essential to consider the depth and breadth of the market for a bond issue. A highly liquid bond market has a large number of active buyers and sellers at all times, creating a market where bonds can be bought or sold quickly with minimal price concessions. Conversely, in a less liquid market, bonds might suffer from wider bid-ask spreads, leading to higher transaction costs and potential issues with accurately pricing bonds (Amihud, Mendelson, & Pedersen, 2012).

Liquidity can evaporate rapidly, particularly in times of financial stress, making it critical for those involved in bond financing to gauge not only the current state of market liquidity but also its resilience. Market shocks can cause investors to sell en masse, potentially leading to a situation where the bond prices drop significantly due to a paucity of buyers, increasing the issuer's cost of capital (Brunnermeier & Pedersen, 2009).

To mitigate liquidity risk, issuers may structure bonds to be more attractive to a broader array of investors. This can include offering higher liquidity premiums, improving covenant terms to offer greater protection to investors, or employing credit enhancements such as letters of credit or bond insurance. Another strategy could involve creating a diversified investor base during the initial bond offering, which can help cushion the impact of individual investor withdrawals on the bond's liquidity.

From the perspective of investors, liquidity risk needs to be factored into investment decisions and portfolio management. The potential need to exit a position swiftly because of unforeseen circumstances could necessitate holding bonds that trade with larger volumes and more frequency or using liquidity risk assessments from rating agencies as part of the decision-making process.

Liquidity risk is a multifaceted issue in the context of project finance bonds, where often the projects are long-term, unique, and carry project-specific risks that do not align with the general market. Assessing this risk requires a clear understanding of market dynamics, investor behaviour, and the fundamental aspects of the bond structure and the underlying project (Fabozzi et al., 2014).

Legal and Regulatory Risks

When project sponsors and capital market professionals embark on bond financing, they must navigate a complex web of legal and regulatory risks which can impact the issuance and lifecycle of a bond. Legal and regulatory risks include compliance with applicable securities laws, tax codes, changes in regulations, and the potential for litigation. These factors must be thoroughly understood and managed to ensure the successful financing of projects through bonds.

Securities laws, at both the federal and state levels, shape the bond issuance process significantly. The Securities Act of 1933 and the Securities Exchange Act of 1934 lay the foundation for the issuance of debt securities, requiring strict adherence to disclosure and registration requirements (Securities and Exchange Commission, 2023). Failure to comply can lead to enforcement actions, including fines and injunctions, which can derail a project's financing and tarnish the reputation of the issuer.

Tax considerations are also a critical facet of legal and regulatory risks. The Internal Revenue Code stipulates various requirements for bonds, particularly tax-exempt bonds, regarding their use and the benefits they confer (Internal Revenue Service, 2022). Changes in tax laws or interpretations can affect the value and attractiveness of bonds to investors, influencing their viability as a financing tool.

In addition to these considerations, the bond market is subject to evolving regulations which can introduce new compliance obligations or modify existing ones. For example, post-financial crisis reforms such as the Dodd-Frank Wall Street Reform and Consumer Protection Act brought significant changes to the financial regulatory landscape, impacting bond issuers and investors alike (Cornett et al., 2020). Staying abreast of such changes is crucial for all parties involved in bond financing.

Lastly, there is the risk of litigation, which can be initiated by stakeholders for reasons such as misrepresentation, non-disclosure, or breach of contract terms. The costs associated with defending against such lawsuits, both in financial and reputational terms, can be substantial and can affect the project's return on investment.

Overall, a comprehensive understanding of legal and regulatory risks is essential. Diligent adherence to relevant laws and regulations, along with proactive risk management strategies, can mitigate these risks, thereby enhancing the prospects for successful bond-financed projects.

Chapter 8:
Structuring Bonds for Project Finance

Effective structuring of bonds is critical to ensure the success and viability of financing large-scale projects. This chapter dives into the details of tailored bond structuring, specifically for project finance, and the strategic considerations that play pivotal roles in enhancing the attractiveness of bonds to investors while mitigating inherent risks.

Secured vs. Unsecured Bonds

One of the foundational decisions in the structuring process involves determining whether the bonds will be secured by specific assets or unsecured, which implies a general claim against the issuer. Secured bonds, often preferred for project finance due to the enhanced assurance they provide to bondholders, are backed by collateral such as property or equipment. In contrast, unsecured bonds are exclusively backed by the creditworthiness of the issuer and often carry higher interest rates to compensate for the increased risk (Fabozzi, 2018).

Senior vs. Subordinate Debt

The hierarchy of debt repayment is another crucial element to be considered when structuring bonds. Senior debt is prioritized over subordinate (or junior) debt for repayment in the event of default or bankruptcy. Typically, senior bonds are viewed as less risky and thus can be issued with lower yields. Subordinate bonds, offering higher yields, appeal to investors with a higher risk appetite. It is important to balance these tiers to optimize the cost of capital while ensuring marketability (Moles et al., 2015).

Tailoring for Time Horizon and Risk Profile

Project finance bonds must align with the expected life span and cash flow patterns of the underlying project. The bond's maturity should reflect the time horizon over which the project can generate returns. Moreover, bonds can be structured with amortizing schedules that align with projected revenue, facilitating repayment in keeping with the project's operational dynamics. Ultimately, the risk profile of the project influences whether the bond terms should be conservative or aggressive; a higher risk may necessitate stronger covenants and guarantees to reassure investors (Esty, 2004).

In conclusion, properly structuring bonds for project finance encompasses choices regarding security, debt seniority, maturity alignment, and risk considerations. These choices shape the bond's appeal to investors and impact the project sponsor's financial obligations, playing a pivotal role in a project's solvency and success.

Secured vs. Unsecured Bonds

In the intricate realm of project finance, the distinction between secured and unsecured bonds forms the bedrock of an issuer's debt obligation and significantly influences both risk assessment and investment appeal. As participants in the capital markets meticulously align financial structuring with the objectives and risk profiles of specific projects, distinguishing the characteristics and implications of secured and unsecured debt instruments becomes an important endeavour.

Secured bonds constitute a pivotal class of debt financing mechanisms wherein the borrower pledges collateral to guarantee the repayment of the bond. This collateral—often in the form of property, equipment, or other tangible assets—serves as a safety net for investors, for it can be seized and liquidated in case of default, thereby reducing potential losses (Fabozzi, 2007). In the context of project finance, such secured bonds are further buttressed by the specific assets or cash flows of the project, tying the security of the investment directly to the project's performance. One quintessential example is the revenue bond, whereby the cash flows generated from the funded project are exclusively allotted to debt service, rendering a non-recourse to the broader credit of the issuer (Yescombe, 2013).

Unsecured bonds, conversely, lack the backstop of specific collateral and are therefore solely underpinned by the general creditworthiness and reputation of the issuer. As such, they expose investors to higher risk since, in the event of insolvency, they stand behind secured debt holders in the priority queue for repayment. Known as 'debentures' in certain jurisdictions, these instruments rely heavily on the issuer's credit rating, making the due diligence and assessment processes undertaken by rating agencies particularly salient (Esty, 2004). Subsequently, unsecured bonds often bear higher interest rates to compensate for the elevated risk profile.

When structuring bonds for project finance, the choice between secured and unsecured must be judiciously examined in light of the project's risk characteristics, the issuer's balance sheet, and the appetite of the potential investor base. Secured bonds may offer reduced financing costs and appeal to risk-averse investors, while unsecured bonds offer greater flexibility for issuers and are potentially more attractive to investors seeking higher yields.

It's critical to understand that the demarcation between secured and unsecured bonds not only affects the cost of capital and the investor base but also influences the legal structure and the contractual covenants that govern the bond issuance. For project sponsors and bankers, it is paramount to ensure that the structure chosen aligns with the strategic objectives of the project and the risk mitigants in place. This alignment enables optimal financing conditions and enhances the project's financial viability, thereby contributing to its success.

Senior vs. Subordinate Debt

In the context of structuring bonds for project finance, a pivotal consideration is the debt hierarchy, most notably the distinction between senior and subordinate debt. This stratification of debt plays a critical role in both the risk profile of an investment and the subsequent rights of creditors in the event of default or bankruptcy (Fabozzi, 2013).

Senior debt, as the name implies, takes precedence over other types of debt and obligations. It is generally secured by collateral, which might include real estate, equipment, or other tangible assets associated with the project. Should the project undergo financial distress, senior debt holders are the first in line to be repaid from the liquidation of the secured assets. Due to this preferential position, senior bonds are seen as lower risk, which typically translates to lower yields when compared to subordinated options. These characteristics make senior debt an appealing choice for conservative investors, such as insurance companies and pension funds (Esty, 2003).

Subordinate debt, on the other hand, occupies a lower tier in the repayment hierarchy. Often referred to as junior debt, it stands behind senior debt in terms of repayment priority during insolvency proceedings. Given the heightened risk, holders of subordinate bonds commonly demand higher interest rates to compensate for the additional risk borne. Subordination can arise contractually or structurally. Contractual subordination is established through the terms of the agreement, whereas structural subordination occurs due to the issuer's position within a corporate group structure—a parent company's debt might be considered senior to that of its subsidiary (Dammon et al., 2001).

This structural hierarchy can be highly influential in the pricing and desirability of bonds issued for a project. Senior bonds, with their lower risk, may attract more conservative and risk-averse investors. Conversely, subordinate bonds can be more attractive to speculative investors looking for higher returns despite the increased possibility of default. Crucially, the mix of senior and subordinate debt issued can significantly affect the overall cost of capital for a project and, thus, its financial viability.

The distribution of risks is not only relevant to investors but also affects the dynamics of the bond issue itself. For instance, a project finance endeavour heavily laden with subordinate debt might face hurdles in attracting investment or may need to offer substantial risk premiums. Additionally, rating agencies, which assess the creditworthiness of the bond issue, often assign higher ratings to senior debt instruments relative to their subordinate counterparts due to their superior claim on assets (Moody's Investors Service, 2016).

In summary, the dichotomy between senior and subordinate debt is integral to the structure and strategy of bond financing in project finance. It draws a clear line among investors in terms of payment priority, risk, and potential return. Careful planning regarding the proportion and terms of each type can optimize the capital structure for the project's specific risk profile and funding needs.

Tailoring for Time Horizon and Risk Profile

Successfully structuring bonds to finance projects involves a meticulous consideration of the time horizon and risk profile specific to the initiative in question. Each project has its own unique set of cash flow projections, anticipated life span, and risk factors which must be taken into account when designing the bond offering (Fabozzi, 2018).

For **time horizon**, bonds can be structured to match the expected duration of the project's revenue-generating phase. Long-term infrastructure projects, for example, might be best served by longer-dated bonds that mature over several decades, providing a match between the financing obligations and the inflow of funds from the completed project (Esty, 2004). On the contrary, shorter ventures such as technology-based initiatives may necessitate shorter maturities that align with rapid changes in the industry and swifter revenue realization.

When it comes to **risk profile**, projects with higher risk may require bonds with higher yields to compensate investors for the additional perceived risk, which reflects in the project's creditworthiness. For higher-risk projects, the structure might include features such as higher coupon rates, offering yield premiums, or employing credit enhancements such as third-party guarantees or reserve funds (Kerzner, 2017). Conversely, projects with a lower risk profile can often issue bonds with lower yields, reflecting the stronger credit ratings and lower default risk associated with these types of projects.

The structuring process also includes the selection of *secured or unsecured bonds*, and the positioning of *senior or subordinate debt—* decisions which are intricately connected to the project's risk profile. Secured bonds, backed by specific assets of the project, might be more appealing to investors concerned about the potential risks of a new project. In contrast, if the project shows strong fundamentals and secure revenue streams, unsecured bonds might be an attractive offer, potentially lowering the cost of capital for the project (Yescombe, 2007).

Assessing the project's characteristics to determine the optimal balance between risk and return for both the issuer and investors is critical. Sponsors and financial advisors need to employ rigorous financial modelling, consider historical data, industry benchmarks, and rating agency assessments to ensure the bond structure is fit for purpose.

Chapter 9:
Bond Pricing Mechanisms

In channelling the discussion towards the spine of bond market operations, we must delve into an intricate aspect of the bond issuance process—the conception and evolution of bond pricing mechanisms. The pricing of bonds is a sophisticated dance of numerical precision and financial intuition, underpinned by both static figures and volatile market sentiments. Project sponsors, bankers, insurance professionals, and all capital market participants must have a keen understanding of how the subtle mechanisms of bond pricing can influence the marketability and success of bond issuances for project financing.

Interest Rate Environments

The environment of interest rates is foundational to any discussion on bond prices. At a surface level, bond pricing seems elementary: A bond's price inversely correlates with interest rates. As rates rise, new bonds are issued with heftier coupons, tipping older bonds with lower coupons to depreciate. In reverse, a rate decline spruces up the value of existing bonds. Yet, this is merely a basic outline; nuances come into play considering the maturity and the coupon of the bond in question (Fabozzi, 2014).

Moving beyond this inverse relationship, it's crucial to think about how interest rates react to monetary policies, economic data, and investors' sentiments (Fabozzi, 2014). These dimensions add layers of complexity when assessing the impact of interest rates on a bond's price.

Yield Curves and Bond Valuation

The yield curve is a formidable tool, displaying the yields across various maturities for similar credit quality bonds, creating a spectrum that suggests the market's views on future interest rates and economic activity. Market participants read yield curves as narratives that detail economic indicators; for instance, an upward sloping curve tends to signal economic expansion, while an inverted one may forebode a recession (Tuckman & Serrat, 2021).

To price a bond, one must not only look at present yield curves but also consider the bond's future cash flows discounted back at the appropriate spots on the curve. This process ensures that the price reflects both the time value of money and the creditworthiness of the issuer (Tuckman & Serrat, 2021).

Spread Analysis

Spread analysis provides additional layers to the bond's pricing mechanism, evaluating the difference in yield between a bond and its benchmark. This spread is influenced by the credit risk, liquidity risk, and maturity. It encapsulates the market's perception of the additional risks associated with a particular bond over a supposed risk-free alternative. Thus, spreads fluctuate as market conditions and perceptions about risk change (Tuckman & Serrat, 2021).

Considering spreads, investors can gauge the attractiveness of a bond in comparison to others within the same or different categories of credit quality. This vigilance in spread analysis aids sponsors and investors in making informed decisions about the pricing and purchasing of bonds.

The intricate dance of bond pricing requires a harmonious combination of understanding current interest rate environments, interpreting yield curves appropriately, and conducting thorough spread analysis. As we have untangled the tapestry of bond pricing mechanisms, project sponsors and financial professionals are equipped to more effectively gauge the right moment and method to enter the market, ensuring optimized funding costs and risk mitigation.

Interest Rate Environments

Understanding the impact of interest rate environments is critical in the context of bond pricing mechanisms. These rates are primarily determined by the central monetary authority of a country—for instance, the Federal Reserve in the United States—and serve as a key influence on the bond markets. Variations in the interest rate environment can affect both the issuance and valuation of bonds significantly, being inherently tied to the prevailing economic conditions (Fabozzi, 2018).

When interest rates are low, the cost of borrowing decreases, which can lead to an increase in bond issuances as companies and governments find it more attractive to raise capital through debt. Conversely, in a high-interest-rate environment, the cost of borrowing increases, potentially leading to a decrease in bond issuances. The prevailing interest rates at the time of issuance will directly impact the coupon rate that is set for a bond, which is the interest rate the issuer promises to pay bondholders. This coupon rate has to be competitive with current interest rates to attract investors (Gitman et al., 2017).

For investors, the interest rate environment plays a vital role in bond valuation. Newly issued bonds must offer yields that are commensurate with interest rates in the broader market. If rates rise after a bond is issued, its price generally falls as the bond becomes less attractive compared to newer issues that offer higher yields. Similarly, if market rates fall, existing bonds with higher coupons become more valuable, leading to an increase in price. Hence, the risk of interest rate fluctuations, also known as interest rate risk, is a significant concern for both issuers and investors alike (Fabozzi, 2018).

Project sponsors, bankers, and capital market professionals must have a keen understanding of these dynamics to effectively price bonds and decide upon the optimal timing for bond issuance. They must assess the current and expected future state of interest rates in the context of the economic cycle, monetary policy, and inflation expectations. Managing this interest rate risk can be crucial, as shifts in rates can markedly influence financing costs and investment returns. Hedging strategies, such as interest rate swaps and options, are often employed to mitigate the negative impact of rising rates on a bond's value over time (Madura & Fox, 2011).

This section has outlined the fundamental ways in which interest rate environments affect bond pricing mechanisms. It sets the stage for understanding other factors that influence bond valuation, such as yield curves and spread analysis, which are explored in subsequent sections.

Yield Curves and Bond Valuation

In the field of bond issuances and project finance, one of the essential concepts is the yield curve and its implications for bond valuation. Understanding how yield curves work, how they relate to interest rates, and their impact on bond pricing can provide valuable insights for project sponsors, bankers, insurance professionals, and capital market experts. This section aims to provide a comprehensive understanding of the relationship between yield curves and bond valuations.

The yield curve is a graphical representation that shows the yields on debt for a range of durations, thus providing a snapshot of how market participants view the future evolution of interest rates (Fabozzi et al., 2012). Depending on market factors, yield curves can take various shapes — normal, inverted, or flat. A standard yield curve, which is upward-sloping, suggests that longer-term bonds have a higher yield compared to short-term bonds. This trend reflects the higher risk associated with long-term bonds, requiring higher returns for investors willing to accept such risks. Conversely, an inverted yield curve, which is downward sloping, suggests that short-term bonds yield more than longer-term bonds, indicating potential economic downturns (Estrella & Mishkin, 1997).

Bond valuation, or what determines the fair price of a bond, is closely linked to yield curves. The fair price of a bond is the present value of its future cash flows, the coupon payments, and the bond's face value at maturity, discounted at an appropriate rate of return or yield (Damodaran, 2012). The appropriate yield to discount a bond's cash flows, in turn, can be obtained from the yield curve for different maturities. Therefore, yield curves play a critical role in computing the fair value of a bond. The relationship between bond prices and yields is inversely proportional; as yields increase, bond prices decrease and vice versa.

Movements in yield curves significantly impact bond valuation. A shift in the yield curve will alter discount rates, thereby influencing bond prices. For those involved in project finance, understanding these shifts is essential to forecasting bond values effectively and managing interest rate risk. When the yield curve steepens (long-term rates rise faster than short-term rates), long-term bonds may see their prices drop faster than short-term bonds, making it a critical consideration for bond portfolio management.

Armed with this understanding, project sponsors, bankers, and related professionals can better navigate bond valuation, manage bond portfolios, and optimize project financing strategies. Predicting changes in yield curves and adapting bond valuation models accordingly becomes an invaluable skill in bond pricing and project finance decision-making.

Spread Analysis

Within the context of bond pricing mechanisms, spread analysis is a critical component that determines the yield differential between two classes of debt instruments, typically benchmark government securities and corporate bonds. In project finance, the spreads can reflect the perceived level of risk associated with a specific project or issuer relative to a risk-free rate. This yield spread compensates investors for bearing the additional risk over and above the default risk of a government bond (Fabozzi, 2018).

The spread analysis begins by identifying a benchmark, often a government bond that corresponds in maturity to the corporate or project finance bond being analyzed. By evaluating the credit spreads, investors and issuers can gauge the relative cost of capital for the project. Market conditions, such as liquidity, investor sentiment, and macroeconomic factors, effectively contribute to the widening or narrowing of these spreads (Hull, 2020).

It's important for all stakeholders to understand the determinants of credit spreads. For project sponsors and capital market professionals, spread analysis serves not only as a pricing tool but also as an indicator of risk premium required by the market. This risk premium is influenced by several factors, including the issuer's credit quality, the complexity of the project being financed, the stability of cash flows, any available credit enhancements, and macroeconomic conditions (Choudhry, 2019).

Spread analysis also aids in determining the optimal timing for market entry. Issuers aiming to minimize their cost of capital will pursue financing when spreads are tight, indicating a lower risk premium. Conversely, heightened spreads indicate increased market risk or uncertainty, suggesting it may be prudent to wait for more favourable conditions before issuing bonds. Moreover, insurance professionals may use spread analysis to price bond insurance products accurately.

For professionals involved in structuring bond offerings, understanding and analyzing spreads is crucial for properly tailoring the bond's features, such as coupon rates and maturity profiles, to match investor demand. In doing so, they aim to achieve a balance between cost-effective funding for the project and providing an attractive return for investors.

Finally, spread analysis is not a static discipline. It requires a dynamic approach to account for ongoing changes in market conditions. Continuous monitoring of the spread movements can provide insights into the trending risks in the bond market, allowing professionals to adjust their strategies accordingly. This vigilance is key in deploying effective risk mitigation strategies over the lifecycle of a project's financing.

Chapter 10:
Regulatory Framework for Bond Issuance

The issuance of bonds as a tool for financing projects is framed by a complex system of regulations that ensures transparency, protects investors, and maintains the integrity of the financial markets. Regulations may range from domestic mandates to global standards that affect the operation and efficiency of capital markets. This chapter explores these essential regulatory environments and outlines the compliance requirements specific to project finance within the bond issuance process.

Domestic Regulations

At the national level, bonds are regulated by securities laws and regulations that govern the issuance, trading, and reporting requirements of debt securities. In the United States, the Securities and Exchange Commission (SEC) requires issuers to register their bond offerings, unless an exemption applies, and to provide detailed disclosures to investors through a prospectus. This document includes information about the issuer, the bond's terms, associated risks, and use of proceeds, among other key details (Schwarcz, 2002).

For municipal bonds, issuers must also adhere to regulations such as the Municipal Securities Rulemaking Board (MSRB) rules which set standards for underwriting practices, transparency, and fair dealing (MSRB, 2021). The Dodd-Frank Wall Street Reform and Consumer Protection Act further introduced municipal advisors who must be registered and are tasked with ensuring the municipalities' interests are safeguarded during the bond issuance process (SEC, 2010).

International Bond Market Regulations

Project financing through bond issuances is increasingly tapping into international markets, thus demanding an understanding of not just domestic, but also international regulatory frameworks. Cross-border issuances must navigate through varying jurisdictional requirements and international securities regulations, such as the International Organization of Securities Commissions (IOSCO) principles, which aim to maintain consistent global standards (IOSCO, 2017).

For Eurobond issuances, which are bonds issued outside of the jurisdiction of any single country and denominated in a currency other than the local currency of the country where it is issued, the regulatory environment may involve multiple countries. The issuers should ensure compliance with the European Union's regulations if selling to European investors, paying close attention to directives like the Markets in Financial Instruments Directive (MiFID) II, which provides a legal framework for securities regulation within the EU.

Compliance Matters in Project Finance

For project sponsors and finance professionals, maintaining strict compliance with the relevant regulatory framework is critical to the success of a bond issuance. It involves a thorough understanding of the reporting requirements, ensuring accuracy of financial disclosures, and meeting ongoing regulatory obligations such as continuing disclosures, which are part and parcel of the post-issuance responsibilities. Non-compliance can lead to legal sanctions, fines, and a loss of market confidence, thereby affecting future fundraising efforts (McDonald & Morris, 2020).

Compliance also extends to recent developments, such as anti-money laundering laws and Know Your Customer (KYC) regulations, which necessitate proper due diligence on potential investors and a detailed understanding of the source of their funds. Adherence to these regulations is essential to mitigate legal risks and ensure the integrity of the capital market.

Domestic Regulations

Understanding the domestic regulatory framework is essential for participants in the bond issuance process. Domestic regulations are the cornerstone of the financial legal structure within which bonds are issued, traded, and managed. These regulations aim to ensure market integrity, protect investors, and promote transparency and efficiency in bond markets. Herein, we delve into the nuances of domestic regulations pertinent to bond issuance, which are integral for financiers and the broader capital market community.

In the United States, for instance, the Securities and Exchange Commission (SEC) plays a pivotal role in the regulatory oversight of bonds. The regulatory responsibilities include, but are not limited to, the enforcement of disclosure requirements for bond offerings. These disclosures are outlined in the Securities Act of 1933 and the Securities Exchange Act of 1934. The Acts mandate the provision of comprehensive financial information and risk factors involved, giving investors a clear understanding of the bond's profile before investing. Moreover, the Municipal Securities Rulemaking Board (MSRB) regulates bond offerings by municipalities, ensuring a set of standards is adhered to in the issuance and sale of municipal bonds (SEC, 2020).

Another crucial aspect of domestic regulation is the adherence to anti-fraud and anti-manipulation standards. Regulations such as the Dodd-Frank Wall Street Reform and Consumer Protection Act have introduced measures to improve transparency and accountability in the financial system, including provisions on the over-the-counter derivatives market (related to some bond transactions) and the "Volcker Rule," which restricts certain speculative investment activities by banks (Carpenter & Murphy, 2010).

Furthermore, banking regulators such as the Federal Reserve and the Office of the Comptroller of the Currency (OCC) impose capital requirements that can influence a bank's decision to underwrite bond issuances. These requirements are part of a broader set of prudential regulations intended to maintain the stability of the financial system.

At the state level, various securities laws, commonly referred to as "blue sky laws," also impact bond issuances. These regulations vary by state and can affect the issuance process through merit reviews, filing requirements, or investment qualifications, adding another layer of complexity to the domestic regulatory landscape (Uriarte, Lisic, & Neal, 2020).

Compliance with these regulations is not optional, and non-adherence can lead to severe repercussions including fines, litigation, and damage to reputations. To navigate this complex regulatory environment, issuers often employ legal advisors and compliance experts who provide guidance on the fulfilment of all legal requirements. This is particularly critical given that domestic regulations are subject to regular updates and reforms, which require issuers and their partners to stay abreast of the latest legal mandates and interpretive guidance issued by regulatory bodies.

In conclusion, domestic regulations form an elaborate tapestry that governs every step of the bond issuance process. From pre-issuance documentation and disclosures to trading practices and post-issuance compliance, each regulatory aspect ensures a fair, efficient, and transparent bond market. Professionals working within the milieu of project finance must diligently adhere to these regulations to orchestrate a successful bond issuance.

International Bond Market Regulations

When considering the issuance of bonds on an international scale, an understanding of the regulatory environment that governs these markets is essential for bankers, project sponsors, insurance professionals, and all parties involved in capital markets. International regulations play a crucial role not only in the initial offering and sale of bonds but also in their ongoing reporting and compliance. The patchwork of international regulations adds layers of complexity that must be navigated to ensure successful project financing through bond issuance.

Each country has its own set of regulations that govern the issuance and trade of bonds within its jurisdiction. However, for bonds that are to be marketed internationally, issuers must comply with a multitude of international regulations and standards. Key among these are the International Organization of Securities Commissions' (IOSCO) objectives and principles of securities regulation, which provide a benchmark for a robust regulatory system (IOSCO, 2020). Adherence to these principles ensures investor protection, fair and transparent markets, and the reduction of systemic risk.

In addition to IOSCO principles, the European Union's Market in Financial Instruments Directive (MiFID) and the U.S. Securities and Exchange Commission (SEC) regulations also strongly influence the international bond markets (European Parliament & Council, 2014; SEC, 2020). Issuers looking to attract investors from different regions must ensure that their offerings comply with relevant local laws. For example, bonds sold to U.S. investors must conform to SEC guidelines, which may require registration or fit within an exemption such as Rule 144A for private placements to qualified institutional buyers.

Furthermore, the International Capital Market Association (ICMA) provides market practices and standards for the international bond market, focusing on fostering good governance and ensuring that the bonds are issued in a manner that promotes transparency and efficiency (ICMA, 2021). ICMA's standards serve as de facto regulations, setting the tone for how international bond transactions should be conducted.

Lastly, it's critical that issuers and their advisors pay close attention to anti-money laundering (AML) regulations and Know Your Customer (KYC) requirements, which are key elements for financial institutions participating in the international bond markets (Financial Action Task Force, 2021). Compliance with AML and KYC requirements is not only a legal obligation but also a fundamental component in establishing the integrity of the parties involved and the source of funds utilized in bond transactions.

By comprehensively understanding these regulations and standards, participants in the international bond market can navigate the complexities of cross-border bond issuance, and effectively use bonds as a mechanism to finance their projects while mitigating associated legal and regulatory risks.

Compliance Matters in Project Finance

Ensuring compliance with regulatory requirements is a cornerstone of successful project finance through bond issuance. In the context of project finance, compliance extends beyond adherence to just the legal statutes. It encompasses a thorough understanding of the regulatory framework for bond issuance, an area that has considerable implications for project sponsors, bankers, and all parties involved (Schwartz et al., 2020).

Firstly, project-related bonds are frequently subject to an array of regulations that govern their issuance, trading, and reporting procedures. In the United States, for example, the Securities and Exchange Commission (SEC) plays a pivotal role in enforcing regulations that protect investors, including those investing in bonds to finance projects. The Municipal Securities Rulemaking Board (MSRB) also lays down rules for municipal securities, which are often used in project financing for public infrastructure (Smith & Wesson, 2019).

Moreover, the compliance landscape becomes more complex when bond issuances cross borders. International regulatory bodies, such as the International Organization of Securities Commissions (IOSCO), establish principles that harmonize cross-border project finance activities. Project sponsors must navigate these alongside bilateral agreements and frameworks that govern international bond market practices (Johnson, 2021).

From a compliance perspective, the structure of the bond itself must be scrutinized. Project finance bonds may come with specific terms regarding the use of proceeds, reporting requirements, and covenant provisions. Ensuring these terms are in compliance with both local and international regulations requires due diligence and often the guidance of specialized legal counsel.

Furthermore, post-issuance, the project sponsors are obligated to maintain ongoing compliance. This involves regular financial reporting, disclosure of material events that could affect bond repayment, and, where applicable, the maintenance of a certain credit rating. Failure to comply can result in severe penalties, including fines and reputational damage, as well as increased costs of capital for future projects.

In summary, the meticulous monitoring of regulatory requirements is not just a legal obligation but forms the fundamental basis for the credibility and viability of the bond-issuance process. Proper guidance and adherence to these regulations can help mitigate risks associated with legal or regulatory infractions, which can have substantial financial and operational ramifications for the project under finance (Schwartz et al., 2020).

Chapter 11:
Environmental, Social, and
Governance (ESG) Bonds

In recent years, there has been a significant shift in how investors and stakeholders evaluate the impact of their investments. This shift has given rise to the importance of Environmental, Social, and Governance (ESG) considerations in investment decisions. Correspondingly, the market for ESG bonds has seen remarkable growth, as these instruments allow project sponsors to target investments that are not only financially viable but also align with broader sustainability goals.

Green Bonds

Green Bonds are designed to fund projects that have positive environmental outcomes. These initiatives may include renewable energy projects, pollution prevention, sustainable water management, and climate change adaptation. Green Bonds bear testament to the issuer's commitment to environmental sustainability and often come with the promise of project-specific transparency in the use of funds (Kidney et al., 2021). For instance, an issuer might provide detailed reports on the environmental impact achieved through the financed project.

Social Bonds

Social Bonds focus on projects that aim to address or mitigate social issues. This can cover a wide range of objectives, such as providing affordable housing, enhancing food security, or promoting socioeconomic advancement and empowerment. Similar to Green Bonds, Social Bonds require transparency and accountability from issuers, ensuring that the capital raised is used for its intended purpose (Best & Harji, 2021).

Sustainability Bonds

Sustainability Bonds are an innovative financial tool that combines the objectives of Green and Social Bonds. These bonds finance projects that achieve both environmental and social benefits. This dual focus allows for a more comprehensive approach to sustainability and opens up opportunities for projects that may not fit neatly into the category of solely green or social. Like their counterparts, Sustainability Bonds typically require issuers to report on the outcomes to ensure that the projects deliver on their ESG promises.

The proliferation of ESG bonds is reflective of a broader societal push towards sustainable development. These bonds provide an avenue for project sponsors to demonstrate their commitment to responsible business practices while also appealing to an investor base that is increasingly conscious of the social and environmental implications of their financial choices. As these securities continue to gain traction, they offer a promising avenue for aligning capital market activities with global sustainability goals.

The success and reliability of ESG bonds, however, hinge on robust frameworks for identifying, verifying, and reporting on ESG outcomes. As such, it is incumbent upon capital market professionals to understand the specific requirements associated with ESG bonds in order to effectively support clients and stakeholders in their endeavours (ICMA, 2021).

Green Bonds

Green bonds represent a critical category within the spectrum of ESG bonds, playing a vital role in mobilizing funds for projects with environmental benefits. Introduced to the financial market more than a decade ago, green bonds have been especially influential in financing renewable energy, energy efficiency, pollution prevention, sustainable land use, and clean transportation ventures. As a reflection of their commitment to environmental sustainability, these bonds are designed to align investment portfolios with climate objectives and reassure investors about the positive impact of their capital (Flammer, 2021).

When a green bond is issued, the proceeds are earmarked for use in eligible green projects. Determining what qualifies as a green project usually adheres to guidelines such as the Green Bond Principles set forth by the International Capital Market Association (ICMA). These principles provide a voluntary framework detailing the use of proceeds, project evaluation and selection, management of proceeds, and reporting (ICMA, 2018). Consequently, green bonds require a transparent and rigorous process of verification to ensure that the funds are deployed towards genuinely sustainable and environmentally friendly projects.

Risk mitigation strategies for green bonds, much like any bond, include thorough due diligence of the proposed green projects and independent reviews or second-party opinions to authenticate the environmental impact. External reviews often, therefore, become a pivotal component in increasing investor confidence and ensuring compliance with green criteria. An ESG rating, provided by reputable agencies, can be a useful metric to assess the sustainability factor and the potential environmental benefits of projects associated with green bonds (Krosinsky & Robins, 2019).

Despite the clear environmental purpose, green bonds are subject to the same financial risks as traditional bonds, including market, credit, liquidity, and legal and regulatory risks. Therefore, banking and financial professionals must exercise due diligence and incorporate a comprehensive risk assessment in the structuring and pricing of green bonds. The role of credit enhancements, such as insurance or guarantees, is also pivotal in mitigating risk and enhancing the bond's creditworthiness.

For project sponsors and capital market professionals, understanding the nuances of green bond issuance is crucial for aligning financial models with environmental goals. The integration of ESG factors into the issuance process not only supports sustainable development but also offers an opportunity to tap into a growing market of environmentally-conscious investors. Thus, green bonds serve as a testament to the synergy between financial viability and environmental responsibility, laying down a blueprint for future ESG-focused financing instruments.

Social Bonds

Within the framework of Environmental, Social, and Governance (ESG) bonds, social bonds emerge as a vital tool for addressing societal challenges through capital markets. The primary objective of social bonds is to raise funds for projects that have a positive social impact, particularly for target populations such as those experiencing socioeconomic disadvantages, underrepresented communities, or areas affected by hardship (Ehlers & Packer, 2020).

For stakeholders in finance, social bonds present an opportunity to align investment strategies with social responsibilities, thereby creating avenues that cater to human capital development, community advancement, and equitable growth. This type of bond typically funds projects spanning affordable housing, education, healthcare, and employment initiatives, among others.

The issuance of social bonds follows a structure akin to traditional bonds, but with a focused emphasis on the social outcomes of the funded projects. These bonds are usually scrutinized by third-party entities to ensure that the proceeds are allocated towards their specified social causes, which is critical for maintaining investor trust and credibility (ICMA, 2021). The proceeds from social bond issuances are often segregated in dedicated accounts to enhance transparency and enable investors to track the deployment of funds towards social projects.

Risk mitigation in social bonds is multifaceted, addressing not only financial risk but also social performance risk. Bond issuers have to frequently report on both financial performance and the social impacts of the funded projects. This includes measurements like the number of beneficiaries, the quality of services provided, and the breadth of community engagement. Such reporting allows investors to assess the social returns on their investments in addition to conventional financial returns.

As the market for ESG bonds grows, the significance of social bonds is underscored by the increasing awareness and demand from investors for products that yield both financial returns and social benefits. By fostering social advancement and demonstrating the scalability of impact investment, social bonds stand out as a distinguished class within the broader spectrum of ESG financial instruments (Krosinsky & Purdom, 2019).

Sustainability Bonds

Within the broader landscape of Environmental, Social, and Governance (ESG) bonds, sustainability bonds emerge as a vital instrument for stakeholders looking to support environmentally and socially responsible projects. As its name suggests, sustainability bonds are debt securities where the proceeds are exclusively applied to finance or refinance a combination of both green and social projects.

Chapter 12:
Innovative Bond Structures

The landscape of project finance is continuously evolving with the emergence of innovative bond structures. In this chapter, we examine several of these structures that enable project sponsors, bankers, and capital market professionals to access funding mechanisms tailored to their unique financing needs. With an emphasis on adaptability and risk management, these instruments represent the leading edge of bond market innovation.

Project Bonds

Project bonds are a dynamic funding tool utilized specifically for financing large-scale infrastructure and industrial projects. These bonds are often structured with a keen focus on permitting investors to invest directly in the project's cash flows, which are segregated from the corporate sponsor's balance sheet (Fabozzi et al., 2016). The bankruptcy-remote feature of project bonds curtails the parent company's liabilities while offering investors a sense of security backed by actual project assets. Typically, the issuance of project bonds is linked to a specific revenue-generating project, such as a toll road or a power plant, and their repayment is predominantly contingent on the project's success.

Infrastructure Bonds

Infrastructure bonds serve to channel investments into essential public sector and public utility infrastructure. These bonds often benefit from governmental support, either through direct guarantees or by the granting of tax-exempt status, which makes them particularly attractive to certain classes of investors (Rajaraman, 2003). They align investors' needs for stable, long-term returns with society's need for sustainable infrastructure development. Innovations in the structuring of these instruments can include private participation where the bonds are offered by a public-private partnership, catering to the financial nuances of such arrangements.

Catastrophe Bonds

Catastrophe bonds, or 'cat bonds', are an innovative risk-transfer mechanism designed to mitigate the financial impact of natural disasters and catastrophic events. Instead of the traditional insurance model, they essentially allow insurers to spread their risk to investors, offering higher coupon rates in exchange for the risk that principal repayments might be delayed or foregone if a triggering event occurs (Lane, 2000). Such an arrangement offers potential for not only insurers but also sovereign states and corporations looking to diversify their risk profiles in the face of unpredictable and potentially devastating events.

Throughout this chapter, it's clear that the ambition to innovate within the bond market has led to the tailoring of financial instruments that not only meet the diverse set of objectives of different projects but also adapt to the modern challenges of the financial environment.

Project Bonds

Within the arsenal of innovative bond structures, project bonds stand out as a pivotal tool for financing large scale infrastructure and industrial projects that might not otherwise have access to traditional loan facilities. These bonds are typically issued for the express purpose of funding a specific project, with the expectation that the project's cash flow will serve as the primary source of repayment investors look for when considering the investment (Esty & Megginson, 2003).

Project bonds differ from conventional corporate or government securities in that they are secured by the project's assets and future revenues rather than the issuer's entire balance sheet (Kerzérho & Lafleur, 2015). This specificity provides a clear visibility on the risk-return profile for the potential investors and allows project sponsors to access capital without spreading the risk across their other operations.

The structuring of a project bond requires meticulous attention to eliminating or mitigating risks to make the bond attractive to investors. Credit enhancement techniques, such as third-party guarantees, letters of credit, or reserve funds, are often used to achieve investment-grade ratings (Yescombe, 2007). These higher ratings mitigate investor concerns about the possibility of project failure and serve to appease the scrutinous eyes of risk-averse capital providers.

Additionally, the lifecycle of a project bond can be complex, requiring stringent adherence to covenants and other contractual obligations that cushion bondholders against potential project uncertainties. The bond indenture typically details these protective measures, requiring the project to meet certain financial and operational benchmarks (Schwartz et al., 2010).

For capital market professionals and project sponsors, it's crucial to understand the nuanced coupling between project bonds and the underlying assets. The bond's yield often reflects the project's risk profile, with investors demanding higher returns for projects perceived as riskier. This makes the pricing mechanism of project bonds an exercise in balancing investor returns with project viability.

In summary, project bonds present an innovative avenue for project finance, one that allows for a tailored approach to funding large-scale ventures. Navigating the complexities of bond issuance, ensuring compliance with legal and regulatory requirements, and engaging in strategic marketing are essential steps for the successful implementation of project bonds within the broader project finance landscape.

Infrastructure Bonds

Infrastructure bonds represent a vital category within innovative bond structures, designed to finance public works like roads, bridges, schools, and utilities, which are crucial for economic growth and development. Unlike traditional municipal bonds, infrastructure bonds can be issued by both government entities and private corporations, offering a broadening of the investment pool.

These bonds often carry specific features to appeal to investors who are interested in long-term capital projects. They can offer tax advantages, including tax-exempt interest income, which can significantly enhance their attractiveness to certain groups of investors (Fabozzi et al., 2014). Infrastructure bonds are particularly characterized by their secured nature, relying on the project cash flows or dedicated tax streams for repayment, which ideally aligns the long-term nature of the liabilities with the long-term assets they finance.

Risk mitigation is an important consideration in the structuring of infrastructure bonds. Given the extended period of project completion and the time until revenue generation commences, these bonds can be at a higher risk of default during the early stages after issuance. Credit enhancement mechanisms, such as bond insurance or letters of credit, can enhance the creditworthiness of these bonds (Kidwell & Brimble, 2008).

The issuance of infrastructure bonds requires careful consideration of the regulatory framework and market risk factors. Upfront capital costs, ongoing operational expenses, and the regulatory landscape can considerably influence the issuance terms and pricing strategies. A comprehensive due diligence process that entails environmental, social, and governance (ESG) assessments also adds to the complexity of issuing infrastructure bonds, ensuring that projects adhere to sustainable practices (Schäfer, 2016).

With advancing technologies and the growing demand for sustainable infrastructure, these bonds are likely to play an increasingly vital role in the development of future projects. As such, entities must approach infrastructure bond issuance with a sophisticated understanding of their unique features and the market dynamics that affect their performance.

Catastrophe Bonds

In the realm of project finance, Catastrophe Bonds (commonly referred to as "Cat Bonds") present an innovative financial instrument that functions as a high-yield debt offering typically issued by an insurance company. These specialty bonds are designed to raise capital to cover the liability from potential catastrophes, such as natural disasters (Cummins & Lalonde, 2003). Insurers transfer the risk of substantial claims resulting from catastrophic events onto investors, providing a hedge against the risk of significant financial loss.

Catastrophe Bonds are typically structured with a multi-year term, and their principal is at risk if predefined triggers are met triggers such as a certain magnitude earthquake or a hurricane surpassing a defined wind speed. If such a trigger event occurs, investors may lose their principal or part of the interest payments. These bonds are thus intimately intertwined with actuarial calculations and sophisticated models to assess the probabilities of hazard risks (Lane, 2000).

The returns on Catastrophe Bonds are generally correlated with the risk level: the higher the likelihood of the trigger event, the higher the coupon payment to the investor. This decouples the bond's performance from the broader financial markets, making Cat Bonds an attractive diversification instrument for investors. However, it's worth noting that Catastrophe Bonds may also involve event risks unanticipated by the models used at the time of structuring the bonds (Cox, Fairchild & Pedersen, 2000).

For project sponsors and insurance entities, Catastrophe Bonds provide a necessary mechanism to manage risk and acquire reinsurance through the capital markets, which can be more cost-effective than traditional reinsurance. This financial instrument equally represents an essential element of the insurance-linked securities (ILS) market, demonstrating the value of innovative bond structures in today's complex financial ecosystem.

From a capital market professional's perspective, understanding the intricate details involved in Catastrophe Bond calculations, including event definition, probability, and pricing, is crucial. This involves disciplined due diligence and the integration of insights from meteorology, seismology, and risk modelling techniques. A robust structure and transparent trigger mechanism are indispensable for the fair assessment and pricing of these bonds.

Investors interested in allocating resources to Catastrophe Bonds must heed the specialized nature of these instruments. The unique risk-return profile requires a thorough evaluation of the issuances, considering key aspects like the sponsor's creditworthiness, the specific terms of the bond, and the historical frequency and severity of the catastrophes covered.

In conclusion, Catastrophe Bonds stand out as a prominent example of how innovative bond structures can offer solutions for risk management in project finance. With careful execution and management, they can bridge the gap between insurance liabilities and investment opportunities, providing a synergistic benefit for both insurers and the market participants (Lane & Mahul, 2008).

Chapter 13:
Case Studies: Bond-Financed Infrastructure Projects

The previous chapters have methodically built a framework of knowledge surrounding the nuances of bond-financed project structures, identifying both opportunities and inherent risks. Chapter 13 extends this theoretical foundation through the exploration of concrete case studies in bond-financed infrastructure projects. This provides readers with a practical understanding of how theoretical concepts are translated into real-world applications.

Public-Private Partnerships (PPPs)

One of the pillars of infrastructure financing is the Public-Private Partnership (PPP), which encapsulates collaboration between government entities and private sector companies. In a PPP, project bonds are often utilized to fund significant portions of the capital expenditure, thereby mitigating the financial burden on the public sector (Yescombe & Farquharson, 2018). An analysis of a highway development PPP demonstrates the dynamics of shared risk, the influence of credit enhancements on investment appeal, and the role of government guarantees in bolstering investor confidence.

Renewable Energy Projects

Rapidly evolving and policy-driven, the renewable energy sector has seen an uptick in bond-financed projects designed to meet sustainability goals. Renewable energy bonds, typically structured with a green bond classification, have become an instrumental funding tool (Dagoumas & Koltsaklis, 2019). The case study of a large-scale solar farm will illustrate the alignment of investment with environmental objectives, the importance of tax incentives, and the management of intermittent energy supply within the project's financial model.

Transportation Infrastructure

Transportation infrastructure acts as the backbone of economic development. A landmark example is a bond-financed airport expansion. This case study highlights the forecast of passenger growth rates, revenue generation through facility usage fees, and the complex interplay between operational risks and external factors such as regulatory changes (Sullivan, 2017). The implications for bond structure, pricing, and the eventual credit rating allocated to such a transaction will be examined in detail.

In spotlighting PPPs, renewable energy, and transportation infrastructure, this chapter offers a cross-sectional view into the multifaceted approach required in bond-driven project finance. Critical lessons are distilled from each case, augmenting the reader's ability to discern the strategies and frameworks that can be applied to future projects. The case studies affirm that while the core principles of bond issuance remain consistent, the application warrants a tailored strategy resonant with the unique requirements and risk profiles of individual projects.

Public-Private Partnerships (PPPs)

Public-Private Partnerships (PPPs) have emerged as a critical instrument in bridging the gap between the investment needs for infrastructure projects and the limitations of public sector budgets. In the context of bond-financed infrastructure projects, PPPs allow for a strategic alignment of interests between public entities seeking infrastructure development, and private investors seeking predictable returns.

In a PPP model, the government entity typically contributes to the project through either direct funding, in-kind assets, or by providing non-financial support such as regulatory permissions and guarantees. On the other side, private sector participants finance a portion of the costs through equity and debt, with project finance bonds being a pivotal component of the latter. These bonds give investors a chance to participate in infrastructure development, often with a secured interest in the project's revenues.

One advantage of PPPs is the distribution of risks. PPP contracts usually include mechanisms that allocate risks among partners in a way that each participant manages the risks they're best equipped to handle. For instance, construction risks may be assigned to the private partner with expertise in the area, while the public sector could deal with regulatory risks (Yescombe, 2014). This balanced risk-sharing encourages more investment into essential projects and can lead to increased efficiencies and innovation in project design, construction, servicing, and maintenance.

A common structure seen in PPPs involves creating a special purpose vehicle (SPV) which is responsible for the project's execution and financing. The SPV issues bonds to finance the project's development, offering investors security through a direct claim on revenues generated by the infrastructure once operational, such as tolls from a bridge or fees from a water treatment facility. The cash flows from these revenues must be carefully assessed and projected to ensure the financial viability of the project and the adequacy of debt service coverage (Esty, 2004).

Bond financing within PPPs presents benefits such as potentially lower borrowing costs compared to traditional financing measures and accessibility to a broader investor base, including institutional investors. Moreover, bond issuance in PPPs can incorporate conditions or features that protect investors, such as reserve funds or guarantees, which can be particularly appealing for long-term investments in infrastructure.

However, PPPs are not without challenges. They often involve complex contractual arrangements and require a high level of coordination between public and private entities. Additionally, PPPs may expose investors to project performance risks that are not typically present in conventional public infrastructure projects. Therefore, meticulous due diligence and risk analysis are paramount.

Case studies have shown that successful PPPs hinge on clear, consistent legal and regulatory frameworks, comprehensive planning, and project selection processes, as well as transparent procurement (Iossa & Martimort, 2015). Proper structuring, along with thorough market and feasibility studies, are also essential in attracting the right blend of debt and equity investors to finance these projects.

In conclusion, PPPs in the realm of bond-financed infrastructure projects offer a collaborative path forward for addressing the significant infrastructure needs of modern society. When designed and executed effectively, PPPs can enable the timely completion of projects while providing financial opportunities and risk-adjusted returns for investors.

Renewable Energy Projects

Renewable energy projects are increasingly utilizing the bond market for securing long-term, stable financing. A pivot towards green initiatives and the rising demand for sustainable development have made renewable energy projects a strong candidate for bond financing. This section explores case studies where bonds have been critical in funding renewable energy infrastructure, such as wind farms, solar arrays, and biomass facilities.

The structure of bonds for renewable energy projects needs to carefully address the inherent risks associated with energy production, technological development, and regulatory changes. For example, to mitigate the risk of technological obsolescence, bonds can be designed with a shorter maturity, aligning with the rapid evolution in renewable energy technologies (Kaminker & Stewart, 2012). Moreover, legislative support for renewable energy can add a layer of credit enhancement for such projects, thereby attracting a larger pool of investors (Bloomberg New Energy Finance, 2021).

One illustrative case of successful bond financing in renewables is the issuance of green bonds for a large-scale solar power project. The bonds may help provide capital for the project's initial development, construction, and operational phases. By emphasizing their 'green' credentials, issuers can access a niche market of environmental, social, and governance (ESG)-focused investors, potentially resulting in more favourable terms and lower interest rates (Sartzetakis, 2013).

Furthermore, the development of the project can be phased, with initial bonds covering early-stage risks and subsequent issuances based on project milestones or operational benchmarks. This strategy can reassure investors about the feasibility and progress of the project, thereby maintaining investor confidence and streamlining the financing process.

Mitigation of risks in renewable energy bond financings also includes off-take agreements with creditworthy counterparties, which assure a defined revenue stream over time. Insurance products, such as production guarantees, can safeguard against underperformance of the energy asset, thus enhancing the project's creditworthiness (Zhang, Wang, & Zhou, 2014).

To conclude, the case studies examined reveal that bond-financed renewable energy projects benefit from a combination of strategic bond structuring, government support, and market mechanisms that ensure risk mitigation while capitalizing on renewable energy's long-term growth potential.

Transportation Infrastructure

Within the realm of bond-financed infrastructure projects, transportation infrastructure represents a significant area where project bonds play a crucial role in development and modernization efforts. Transportation infrastructure projects encompass a wide range of initiatives from highways and bridges to airports and mass transit systems, and they often require substantial capital investments for both construction and maintenance over time.

The financing of transportation infrastructure through bonds is generally preferred due to the long-term nature and high upfront costs of these projects. Project bonds, particularly municipal bonds and revenue bonds, are frequently utilized instruments in this context. The revenue generated from transportation projects, such as tolls and transit fares, can often be directly employed to service the debt, making revenue bonds an attractive option for investors seeking lower risk investments (Fabozzi et al., 2017).

An example that exemplifies the utilization of bond finance for transportation infrastructure is the raising of funds for a new highway project. The issuing authority, typically a regional government or a special-purpose entity, issues bonds to investors in order to finance the construction. These project bonds may be designed with various maturities, depending on the estimated cash flows from the highway's operation, and they reflect a detailed analysis of traffic projections and toll revenue estimates (Yescombe, 2014).

Risk mitigation in bond-financed transportation projects is of paramount concern for both sponsors and investors. Credit enhancements, such as bond insurance or the provision of reserve funds, are mechanisms that could be included to improve the credit rating of the issuance and secure favorable interest rates (McKinney, 2019). Moreover, it is essential for project sponsors to conduct comprehensive traffic and revenue studies to anticipate and manage demand risk, addressing concerns over the adequacy of projected cash flows to meet debt service obligations.

Bond-financed transportation infrastructure projects not only serve a public function by enhancing mobility and accessibility but also stimulate economic growth by facilitating trade and commerce. The intricate structure of these bonds requires all parties involved—bankers, project sponsors, insurance professionals, and capital market professionals—to possess a deep understanding of the dynamics of bond issuance and the specificities inherent in transportation infrastructure projects.

Chapter 14:
The Global Bond Market Landscape

In expanding our examination of bonds within project finance, it becomes critical to step back and consider the larger context—the global bond market landscape. The patterns and phenomena within different markets around the world give us insights into the wave of opportunities and challenges that project sponsors and financiers alike may encounter. This chapter presents a comparative analysis of key markets and identifies emerging trends that shape bond financing globally.

Comparative Analysis of Key Markets

The global bond market is a vast and intricate terrain, influenced by diverse economic policies, regulatory frameworks, and market dynamics (Fabozzi, 2018). The United States, through venues such as the New York Stock Exchange, represents the largest single-country bond market, replete with a wide array of corporate and government issues. The depth and liquidity of the U.S. market offer a benchmark for risk and valuation attributable to its established credit rating system and wide investor base.

In Europe, the bond market is shaped by the multiplicity of sovereign issuers within the Eurozone and the regulatory guidance of the European Central Bank. Here, markets balance the sovereign bond issues from the larger economies of Germany and France against those from smaller economies, reflecting a diverse credit risk landscape (Schwarcz, 2020).

Emerging markets, such as those in Southeast Asia and Latin America, present a different picture, where local currency issuances are growing, albeit with heightened perceptions of risk. Extended risk often translates into higher yields, making them potentially attractive for certain investors (Reinhart & Rogoff, 2009). Project sponsors tapping into these markets may need to address currency risk and local regulatory hurdles, factors that can significantly affect bond structuring and pricing.

Emerging Trends in Bond Financing

Trends in global bond financing hint towards a more interconnected and fluid market where innovations in one region rapidly influence others. A prominent trend is sustainable and responsible investment, reflecting an increased appetite for green, social, and sustainability bonds, especially in light of global climate commitments (Flammer, 2021).

Technology's role is another growing trend, with fintech companies facilitating more efficient bond trading and issuance processes. Digitization, including blockchain-based digital bonds, promises to unlock efficiencies and democratize access to the bond markets by reducing barriers and costs of entry (Gomber et al., 2017).

Additionally, amidst the global economic uncertainty of recent years, there has been increased focus on the enhancement of liquidity management and the issuance of bonds with features such as longer maturities or more flexible covenants to cater to the changing risk appetites of investors.

Understanding these global nuances and trends is not merely an academic exercise—it empowers practitioners with the foresight to make well-informed decisions, whether they are structuring a new bond issue, planning a financing strategy, or assessing investment options.

Comparative Analysis of Key Markets

The landscape of global bond markets is as diverse as it is dynamic. Within this vast financial fabric, certain key markets stand out, each possessing distinct characteristics, opportunities, and challenges. The comparative analysis that follows is crucial for practitioners and stakeholders, who must navigate these markets with a comprehensive understanding of their nuances.

In the United States, the bond market is one of the largest and most developed globally. U.S. Treasuries form the backbone of the global financial system, often serving as a benchmark for other assets. Furthermore, the municipal bond market offers a way for local governments to finance public projects while providing investors with tax-exempt income opportunities (Fabozzi et al., 2019). Corporate bonds in the U.S. also present a significant market segment, distinguished by a highly standardized issuance process and a robust regulatory environment.

Across the Atlantic, the European bond market has been shaped by the diverse fiscal policies of its member states and the overarching monetary regulations of the European Central Bank. The Eurobond market, in particular, serves as a major platform for international issuers seeking to reach global investors without being subject to the regulations of a specific country (Schmidt et al., 2016). Sovereign bonds, in some European nations, carry their own risks due to varying creditworthiness, an element critical to consider in project finance.

Emerging markets present an entirely different sphere. Countries like Brazil, Russia, India, China, and South Africa have been garnering more interest from bond investors due to higher yields and growing economic prospects. While these markets offer considerable potential, they also come with greater credit, market, and currency risks (Patel & Sanya, 2018). Local market knowledge and a sound understanding of sociopolitical dynamics are required to mitigate these added risks in project financing.

When comparing these markets, several factors must be weighed, including market size and liquidity, interest rate environment, regulatory complexity, credit risk profiles, and the presence of institutional investors. For project sponsors and financiers, understanding these differences is essential to strategize bond issuances effectively. One must tailor financial structures to the particular market, ensuring compliance with local regulations while optimizing the cost of capital to maximize financial benefits.

Engaging within these diverse markets necessitates a meticulous approach to due diligence, a keen eye for the influence of geopolitical shifts, and a flexible strategy capable of adapting to emerging trends. As the global economic landscape continues to evolve, so too do the dynamics of bond markets, reinforcing the need for a thorough comparative analysis as part of strategic financial planning.

Emerging Trends in Bond Financing

The landscape of global bond financing is constantly evolving, with innovation and regulatory changes shaping the way issuers, and investors engage with the bond market. This section highlights several key emerging trends that are influencing bond financing in a significant way.

One trend gaining traction is the proliferation of **environmental, social, and governance (ESG) bonds**. As awareness and concern for sustainability issues grow, bonds that finance projects with positive environmental or social impacts have become increasingly popular. Green bonds, for example, have witnessed a surge in issuance as they are used to fund renewable energy projects and other environmental initiatives (Climate Bonds Initiative, 2022). Social and sustainability bonds, which finance projects with direct social benefits or a combination of environmental and social benefits, have similarly seen growing interest.

Another trend is the rise of **digital and blockchain-based bonds**. Technological advancements have allowed for enhancements in bond issuance and trading processes, fostering greater transparency and speed. Blockchain technology, in particular, is being explored for its potential to streamline operations and reduce costs associated with bond issuance (Gomber et al., 2021). Digital ledgers can also facilitate real-time tracking of bond ownership and payments.

The evolution of bond structures is also a significant trend. There has been a notable increase in the use of **project bonds** for infrastructure financing, shifting away from traditional bank loans. These bonds are tied to the cash flows of a specific project, providing a mechanism that can attract institutional investors with a long-term investment horizon (Schwartz et al., 2019).

Lastly, amid global economic shifts, there has been a greater focus on **risk mitigation strategies** within bond financing. New bond features, such as contingent convertibles (CoCos) and bonds with warrants, offer issuers the means to manage risk exposure while providing additional incentives for investors. These innovative structures can adjust terms based on the performance of the underlying project and broader market conditions.

These emerging trends reflect the dynamism in the global bond market and the continuous search for more efficient, resilient, and sustainable financing solutions. As these new trends become more embedded in market practices, they will likely influence the standard methodologies discussed elsewhere in this text.

Chapter 15:
Strategic Marketing for Bond Offerings

Having thoroughly explored the intricacies of bond structures, regulations, and the global bond market landscape in prior chapters, we now shift our focus to the quintessential aspect of marketing bond offerings competitively and effectively. Strategic marketing is critical for the successful issuance of bonds, as it serves the purpose of appealing to the right segment of investors and securing the needed capital.

Identifying and Engaging Investors

The success of a bond offering hinges on comprehensive market analysis and investor segmentation. It is essential to understand the motivations and investment criteria of potential bond purchasers. Institutional investors, such as pension funds, insurance companies, and mutual funds, often seek stable, long-term returns and may be more inclined towards high-credit quality bonds (Fabozzi et al., 2020). Contrastingly, hedge funds and other active traders might look for higher-yield, riskier securities for short-term gains. Assessing market conditions, understanding investor appetite, and considering the timing of the issue are fundamental steps in plotting a strategic marketing approach. Additionally, a tailored communication plan that concisely presents the unique selling points of the bond can influence investor interest and favourability towards the offering (Fabozzi et al., 2020).

The Role of Roadshows and Presentations

Roadshows are a pivotal part of bond issuance, establishing direct communication channels between issuers and potential investors. The purpose is to elucidate the investment opportunity, detail the use of proceeds, and provide pertinent information about the bond's features, such as yield, maturity, and covenants. During these presentations, it is critical for issuers, often accompanied by their underwriters, to convey their creditworthiness and the underlying project's potential. This interaction affords an opportunity not only to respond to investor queries but also to build confidence and trust in the bond offering (Morrison & Wilhelm, 2007).

Effective Communication Strategies

Effective communication is indispensable throughout the bond marketing process. Clarity, consistency, and transparency are the pillars on which successful investor relations are established. Project sponsors and their advisory teams need to craft clear and compelling narratives that highlight the strengths of their bond offering while also addressing potential risks. A well-defined strategy includes a robust investor relations platform, timely dissemination of financial information, and maintaining open channels for investor feedback (Hill et al., 2022).

At the core of these strategies lies the necessity to not only align the bond offering with the interests and requirements of the target investor base but also to position it favourably in a competitive market. By understanding investor expectations and preferences, issuers can optimize the terms of the bond, choose the most appropriate communication channels, and execute their marketing strategies effectively.

Identifying and Engaging Investors

For a successful bond offering, it's essential to identify and actively engage the right set of investors. Understanding investors' risk profiles, investment criteria, and expectations can have a significant impact on the marketing strategy of a bond issue. The investor base for bonds can be diverse, ranging from institutional investors, such as pension funds and insurance companies, to individual retail investors.

One primary step in engaging investors is to segment them based on characteristics such as risk tolerance, investment horizon, and income needs. Institutional investors, for example, may be more concerned with the long-term creditworthiness and the sustainable returns of a bond offering (Fabozzi et al., 2014). On the other hand, retail investors may prioritize bonds that are simpler, less risky, and offer tax advantages when applicable.

Mapping out a suitable investor base requires thorough research and an understanding of the current market dynamics. Market research studies, financial databases, and historical investor behaviour offer insights that help in pinpointing potential investors who show a preference or inclination for the bond's characteristics.

Once potential investors are identified, strategic engagement begins with education and transparent communication regarding the project's specifics and the bond's features. Offering bespoke presentations and detailed documentation serve to address most concerns and queries investors might have. Establishing a strong value proposition is key, highlighting how the bond meets investor requirements and stands out within the market (Schwartz & Aronson, 2013).

Engagement efforts continue by fostering relationships through roadshows, one-on-one meetings, and investor conferences. These create platforms for direct interaction, providing opportunities for issuers to build trust and credibility with potential investors (Schwartz & Aronson, 2013). It's critical to keep investors informed and reassured about the bond's performance and the project's progress during the bond life cycle.

To maintain interest and strengthen investor relationships, issuers must ensure regular and open lines of communication post-issuance. This can include scheduled updates, comprehensive reports on project developments, and rapid responses to any changes in project risk profiles.

Engaging investors doesn't only have immediate benefits for the current bond issue but also sets the foundation for future financing activities. It can lead to a loyal investor base willing to participate in additional offerings and recommend the bonds to other potential investors, thus widening the issuer's reach in the capital markets.

The Role of Roadshows and Presentations

Effective marketing is crucial for the success of bond offerings in project finance. A key element in this strategy is the execution of roadshows and presentations, which collectively serve as the investor-facing front of a bond issuance campaign. Roadshows allow issuers, usually represented by senior management and financial officers, to meet with potential investors directly to pitch the bond offering, articulate the investment thesis, and address inquiries (Fabozzi, 2012).

Roadshows and presentations essentially fulfil two main objectives: informing and persuading potential investors. They are a platform to convey the bond's value proposition and the issuer's creditworthiness, reinforcing the findings of credit rating agencies (Moody's Investors Service, 2020). Such events are typically characterized by well-crafted presentations detailing financial projections, growth strategies, underlying risks, and mitigation measures. They provide a narrative beyond the numbers that can strengthen an investor's confidence in the bond offering.

Scheduling and planning the roadshow itinerary requires careful consideration of geographic locations and investor profiles. Issuers aim to reach a broad audience while giving particular attention to institutional investors known for holding sizable bond portfolios. Digital roadshows have also become increasingly common, offering a cost-efficient alternative or supplement to in-person events, expanding global reach and enabling wider access for interested investors (Nguyen & Faff, 2006).

During the roadshow, issuers are expected to present a detailed investment prospectus that includes past performance, management details, future prospects, risk factors, and use of proceeds. This prospectus is a critical component in helping investors make informed decisions about participating in the bond offering (Fabozzi, 2012).

It's also essential for presenters to anticipate and prepare for potential questions from investors. This preparation demonstrates thorough knowledge and can alleviate investor concerns regarding the project's viability and the likelihood of timely interest and principal repayments.

In summary, roadshows and presentations are a strategic tool to attract and engage potential investors in bond offerings. They provide a dynamic and interactive environment that can significantly bolster investor interest and confidence, culminating in the successful placement of bonds in project finance.

Effective Communication Strategies

As stakeholders in strategic marketing navigate the complexities of bond offerings, the pivot to 'Effective Communication Strategies' becomes a cornerstone in shaping investor perceptions and facilitating investment decisions. Amidst the plethora of marketing activities, each requiring meticulous detail and strategic finesse, communication stands out as a vital tool to coherently convey the value proposition of the bond to potential investors. This section elucidates the most impactful communication strategies tailored for bond offerings within the terrain of project finance.

Clear and consistent messaging is the first tentpole of an effective communication strategy (McLean & Ziemba, 2006). For bond offerings, it is essential to create a narrative that encapsulates the project's potential, the security of the investment, and the anticipated returns. This narrative should be consistently reflected across all marketing materials, from the prospectus to investor presentations. The coherence of the message reassures investors of the issuer's credibility and the bond's value.

Furthermore, the communication plan must adapt to the varied spectrum of investors. Some may have a preference for in-depth quantitative analysis, while others might focus on qualitative factors, such as the environmental impact of the project being financed. The communication strategy should be flexible enough to cater both to institutional investors, who may prioritize the minutiae of financial metrics and risk assessments, and to retail investors, whose decisions might be more influenced by the project's social or environmental implications (Baker & Martin, 2011).

Digital channels, especially in the current landscape, play a crucial role in disseminating information broadly and efficiently. A dedicated online portal for the bond offering, alongside the use of email campaigns, social media, and webinars, can maximize outreach and engagement (Wonglimpiyarat, 2014). Interactive tools offer potential investors the opportunity to explore the nuances of the bond offering at their own pace, providing a supportive platform for self-guided discovery that complements more traditional investor meetings and roadshows.

To manage investor relations proactively, issuers must commit to openness and transparency. Regular updates on the project's progress, risks, and any changes in financial projections or assumptions are imperative. During the life of the bond, maintaining a dialogue with bondholders protects the issuer's reputation and may even smooth the path for future financing initiatives. This is particularly essential when faced with project delays or setbacks, where clear communication may help mitigate investor concerns.

In conclusion, strategizing potent communication methods is essential for convincing prospective investors of the worthiness of a bond. The intertwining of lucid narratives, adaptable content, innovative digital platforms, and uncompromising transparency forms a robust framework to propel the marketing efforts of bond offerings to success.

Chapter 16:
Understanding Bond Covenants

The terrain of bond covenants is an essential aspect that safeguards the interests of both bondholders and issuers. Covenants are legally binding clauses embedded within the contractual terms of a bond issuance, designed to protect the capital of investors by ensuring that issuers adhere to specific financial and operational guidelines. In this chapter, we will dissect affirmative and negative covenants, delve into the intricacies of their negotiation and enforcement, and explore the consequences of covenant breaches.

Affirmative and Negative Covenants

Affirmative covenants are contractual obligations requiring the bond issuer to perform certain activities. These may include maintaining financial ratios at specified levels, providing periodic financial reporting, and ensuring the proper maintenance of assets that secure the bond (Smith & Warner, 1979). For instance, an issuer might be required to sustain a specified debt-to-equity ratio or to ensure insurance is up-to-date on assets used as collateral.

In contrast, negative covenants are restrictions that prohibit the issuer from undertaking specific actions. These may encompass limitations on additional borrowing, restrictions on asset sales, or constraints on entering into certain types of transactions. The primary purpose of these negative covenants is to prevent the degradation of the issuer's financial position or acts that could jeopardize the interests of the bondholders (Triantis & Daniels, 1995).

Covenant Negotiation and Enforcement

Covenant terms are often a point of rigorous negotiation between the issuer and the investors, as each party strives to achieve a balance between flexibility and security. Successful covenant negotiation relies on an in-depth understanding of the issuer's business model and the associated risks (Robbins & Chatterjee, 1991). The onus lies both on articulating a robust case for covenant specifics in line with the project's peculiar requirements and on crafting covenants that are acceptable to potential investors.

Enforcement of covenants usually falls under the purview of a trustee or a fiscal agent, who acts on behalf of the bondholders. The trustee monitors the issuer's compliance with the covenants and takes action when a breach occurs. Enforcement mechanisms can include issuing a notice of non-compliance, engaging in discussions to remedy the breach, or taking legal action, depending on the terms agreed upon during the issuance.

The Implications of Breaching Covenants

A breach of covenants can have severe repercussions. A minor infraction may result in a waiver or amendment of the covenants, often accompanied by penalties or fees. However, significant breaches can lead to an event of default, which triggers mechanisms for investors to seek immediate remedy, potentially accelerating the repayment of the bonds. Therefore, crafting and adhering to realistic and prudent covenants is crucial for maintaining the confidence of the investment community and ensuring the ongoing feasibility of projects financed through bond issuance (Esty, 2014).

Affirmative and Negative Covenants

In the realm of bond financing, covenants are promises made by the issuer enshrined within the terms of the bond agreement. These promises are legally binding and are designed to protect the interests of both the bondholders and the issuer. When it comes to project finance, where the financing is typically secured by the project's cash flow and assets, the significance of bond covenants becomes even more pronounced. This section elucidates the two primary types of covenants—affirmative and negative—and their implications for bond issuers and holders in a project finance context.

Affirmative Covenants, also known as positive covenants, require the issuer to undertake specific actions or meet certain benchmarks during the bond's lifetime. These typically include regular financial reporting, maintenance of certain financial ratios (like debt-service coverage ratios), and ensuring the proper maintenance of assets that secure the bond. For instance, a covenant may stipulate the issuer must retain a specific level of insurance coverage on a project (Smith et al., 2021). Such covenants assure the bondholders that the issuer is actively managing the project in a manner that promotes ongoing viability and risk mitigation.

Negative Covenants restrict the issuer from certain activities, thereby limiting behaviour that could compromise the issuer's ability to fulfil its obligations or dilute the bondholders' security. These often include limitations on additional borrowing, restrictions on asset sales, and constraints on dividend payments (Jones & Patel, 2019). Negative covenants are designed to preserve the project's capital base and ensure that cash flows are used to service debt rather than for other potentially risk-enhancing pursuits.

The balance between affirmative and negative covenants is critical to the success of a bond issuance. Too stringent covenants could restrain an issuer's operational flexibility, potentially hampering the project's profitability. Conversely, overly lenient covenants might fail to provide adequate protection to bondholders. Therefore, the negotiation of these covenants is a delicate process, where issuers and bondholders must carefully consider the project's unique risks and rewards (Taylor, 2022).

Bond covenants are pivotal risk management tools, enabling bondholders to monitor and control the behaviour of the issuer and creating a framework within which the project can be executed effectively. For bankers, insurance professionals, and capital market experts, understanding the nature and function of these covenants is vital for conducting due diligence and assessing the quality of a bond issuance.

Covenant Negotiation and Enforcement

Understanding bond covenants is essential for ensuring the fruitful interactions between bond issuers and investors throughout the life of a bond. After navigating through the varied spectrum of covenants in the preceding sections, we now focus on the critical processes of negotiating and enforcing these covenants within the framework of project finance.

At the onset of covenant negotiation, project sponsors and investors lay the groundwork for their financial relationship. Affirmative covenants stipulate the issuer's obligations, reinforcing positive action, such as maintaining certain financial ratios and providing regular financial statements (Watson & Head, 2016). In contrast, negative covenants, often more contentious, limit the issuer's actions to protect the bondholders' interests, like restrictions on additional debt or asset disposal.

The intricacies of covenant negotiation revolve around a finely-tuned equilibrium where issuers aim for operational flexibility while investors seek protection against default risk (Esty, 2004). Sophisticated negotiation strategies often involve advisors who possess intricate knowledge of the bondholder's sentiments, the trajectory of the project, and the pulse of market conditions. These advisors help tailor covenants to fit the unique risk profile of each project finance endeavour, considering factors such as the project's lifespan, revenue generation mechanisms, and underlying asset volatility.

As covenants are formalized, enforcement mechanisms become pivotal for preserving the bond's underlying value and the stakeholders' confidence. Enforcement is a multi-layered concept starting with the monitoring process. Typically, trustees play an intricate role in ensuring adherence to covenants and signalling any deviations to bondholders (Fabozzi et al., 2012).

In instances of covenant breaches, swift corrective actions are imperative for maintaining fiscal discipline and mitigating risks. Sanctions for such breaches can include higher interest rates, remediation plans, or, in extreme cases, acceleration of debt repayment. Establishing clear, enforceable penalties during the negotiation phase is crucial, as the enforcement process relies heavily on predetermined agreements between the involved parties.

Ultimately, the effectiveness of covenant enforcement is contingent upon the meticulous drafting of covenants and the robustness of oversight mechanisms. This underscores the delicate power dynamics between project sponsors seeking growth and flexibility, and bondholders guarding against default risk. The outcome is a detailed contractual framework fostering long-term financial stability and project viability, reinforced by the collective efforts of legal teams, advisors, trustees, and regulators within the project finance landscape.

The Implications of Breaching Covenants

Bond covenants are essential components of the protections afforded to bondholders and play a crucial role in the risk structure of a bond issuance. The implications of breaching these covenants can be significant and varied, both for the bond issuer and the bondholders.

When a covenant breach occurs, it represents a failure to comply with the terms agreed upon during the issuance of the bond, which may lead to a series of legal and financial repercussions (Smith et al., 2020).

A primary consequence of a covenant breach is the potential for bondholders to demand immediate repayment of their investment, often referred to as "**acceleration**" (Miller & Reed, 2018). This action can put severe financial strain on the issuer, particularly if the project being financed is not generating sufficient cash flow to repay the obligation. Acceleration can also trigger cross-default provisions, where a default on one obligation leads to a default on other obligations, potentially throwing the issuer into a financial crisis.

In addition to acceleration, bondholders may seek to enforce their rights through legal action, which can be costly and time-consuming for all parties involved. The ensuing legal battles can erode trust in the bond issuer, damage the issuer's creditworthiness and reputation in the capital markets, and impair the issuer's ability to raise funds in the future (Johnson, 2021).

Furthermore, the breach of covenants can result in credit downgrades by rating agencies, which can increase the cost of borrowing, restrict access to capital, and create a negative perception among investors. The perception of higher risk associated with the bond can lead to a decline in its market value, thereby harming existing bondholders through reduced liquidity and potential capital losses.

For project sponsors and other stakeholders, understanding the implications of breaching covenants is crucial for maintaining fiscal discipline, ensuring project viability, and safeguarding the interests of all parties involved. The management teams must also consider the specific provisions related to waiver or amendment of covenants, which may allow the issuer some flexibility in certain circumstances without triggering a default (Smith et al., 2020).

It is vital for bond issuers to maintain open lines of communication with bondholders, especially when they anticipate or experience difficulties meeting covenant terms. Being proactive in addressing covenant breaches can help mitigate the negative impacts and preserve the relationship with investors, thereby maintaining the integrity of financial and capital markets.

Chapter 17:
Hedging Strategies in Bond Financing

As we pivot from understanding the implications of bond covenants, it's crucial to dive into the tactics employed to mitigate the risks associated with bond financing. Specifically, Chapter 17 zeroes in on hedging strategies that can protect against fluctuating interest rates, currency risks, and credit volatility.

Interest Rate Swaps

An indispensable tool for managing interest rate exposure is the interest rate swap. This financial instrument allows bond issuers to exchange their existing interest rate payments for payments with different characteristics. Typically, this involves swapping from a variable-rate obligation to a fixed-rate obligation, or vice versa, depending on the issuer's assessment of future interest rate movements and their appetite for risk (Tuckman & Serrat, 2011).

Working with these derivatives, entities can achieve more predictable debt service costs, which can be especially beneficial when future cash flow stability is a priority. The goal is to neutralize the risk of rate fluctuations that could adversely impact servicing bond debt, which can be critical for maintaining project budgets and financial forecasts.

Currency Swaps

In projects funded through bonds that generate revenue in multiple currencies or when bonds are issued in a foreign currency, currency swaps are an essential hedging strategy. These agreements permit the exchange of principal and interest payments in one currency for those in another, effectively locking in exchange rates and removing the uncertainty associated with currency fluctuations.

The strategic use of currency swaps can be a guard against exchange rate volatility, ensuring that the debt repayment schedule is not disrupted by adverse currency movements (Arora, 2012). This can be particularly relevant for multinational projects or issuers looking to attract a diverse pool of international investors by issuing debt in currencies other than their domestic one.

Credit Default Swaps

Another layer of risk protection comes in the form of credit default swaps (CDS). A CDS is essentially insurance against the default of a bond issuer. The buyer of a CDS makes periodic payments to the seller, and in return, receives a payoff if the underlying bond defaults (Stulz, 2010). Such instruments cultivate a market of risk-sharing and can influence the perceived creditworthiness of bond issuers.

Project sponsors and other entities engaged in bond financing deploy CDS to manage their credit risk, often leading to improved confidence among investors concerning the probability of default. The ability to transfer credit risk using CDS can have a substantial impact on the cost of borrowing and the overall financial health of projects reliant on bond financing.

Conclusion

Implementing these hedging strategies requires careful consideration of the existing risk profile, cost implications, and alignment with the broader financial strategy of the bond issue. While employing swaps and derivatives can provide significant protection against market uncertainties, it requires a sophisticated approach involving accurate risk assessment and a deep understanding of financial markets.

By incorporating these hedging tactics, project sponsors and financiers can better manage unexpected changes in interest rates, currency values, and credit conditions, leading to a more robust and stable financing environment for sizable and complex projects.

Interest Rate Swaps

Interest rate swaps figure prominently among hedging strategies used in bond financing and serve as a fundamental tool to manage and mitigate interest rate risk. An interest rate swap is a financial derivative contract in which two parties agree to exchange one stream of interest payments for another, based on a specified principal amount. Typically, this involves a swap between fixed-rate and floating-rate interest payments. They provide a way for parties involved in project financing to lock in current interest rates, hedging against potential interest rate volatility that can significantly alter the cost of borrowing over time.

When project sponsors or corporations engage in fixed-to-floating or floating-to-fixed rate swaps, they're effectively reconfiguring the cash flow profile of their debt to align with expectations about interest rate movements, risk appetite, and cash flow objectives. By doing so, a project with a variable-rate debt issuance, uncertain about future interest rate increases, can swap their payments with another entity that wishes to take on this variability in exchange for steady, predictable fixed rate payments (Tuckman, 2012).

In fixed-to-floating rate swaps, a bond issuer with a fixed rate liability can enter into a swap to pay a floating rate, thereby expecting to benefit if rates fall. Conversely, an issuer carrying a floating rate liability might enter into a swap to pay a fixed rate, with the expectation of protecting themselves against rising interest rates (Hull, 2015). Interest rate swaps are particularly valuable in the context of project finance, where the borrowing environment may fluctuate significantly over the duration of the project, impacting the project's financial viability and potential for higher costs or reduced margins.

Utilizing interest rate swaps can lead to potential benefits such as enhanced debt portfolio management, better matching of assets and liabilities, and a reduction in the cost of funds. However, they are not without risks, including counterparty risk where the other party in the swap may default, and basis risk, where the floating rate being paid does not move in perfect correlation with the floating rate being received (Pilbeam, 2010).

Moreover, engaging in interest rate swaps requires continuous monitoring and reassessment. As economic conditions change, the value of the swap itself becomes a variable that needs managing. Professional advice is often sought from financial advisors or derivative specialists to assess the appropriateness of an interest rate swap within the wider financial strategy of the issuing body.

In conclusion, interest rate swaps can be a versatile and effective tool for managing the interest rate exposure inherent in bond financing. They allow project sponsors to mitigate financial risk and achieve a more predictable cost profile for their debt obligations. Considering their complexities and the risks involved, careful structuring and management are imperative to reap their potential benefits while avoiding pitfalls.

Currency Swaps

In the context of bond financing for projects, currency swaps serve as an instrumental hedging strategy to mitigate exchange rate risk. A currency swap is a financial derivative that involves the exchange of principal and interest in one currency for the same in another currency. It is an arrangement between two parties to trade cash flows based on a notional principal amount, which is not effectively exchanged, thus avoiding the need to borrow directly in a foreign market (Moffett, Stonehill, & Eiteman, 2015).

For project sponsors involved in international ventures, the volatility of exchange rates can introduce additional risk to the project's cash flow and overall financial stability. If a project is financed in one currency but generates revenue in another, the mismatch can lead to significant financial exposure. Currency swaps are utilized to convert the debt service requirements of bonds into the project's operating currency, therefore, aligning cash inflows and outflows and creating predictability in cash flows.

An example would be a U.S. company issuing bonds to finance an infrastructure project in Europe. The company could enter into a currency swap agreement with a European counterpart, swapping the dollar debt service payments for euro payments, which aligns with revenue generated from the project. This transaction is notably beneficial as it not only hedges exchange rate risk but can also provide access to more favourable borrowing rates if interest rate differentials exist between the two currencies.

It is essential, however, to approach currency swaps with a thorough understanding of the terms involved. These include the length of the swap, which typically matches the maturity of the bonds, the fixed or floating interest rates used in calculating the periodic cash flows, and the mechanisms for exchanges of principal at the start and end of the contract. Sponsors must also assess the credit risk linked to the counterparty in the currency swap and may necessitate collateral agreements or other credit enhancement techniques to mitigate this risk (Pilbeam, 2013).

The accounting for currency swaps must be scrupulous, with attention to both the initial recognition and subsequent measurement of the swap according to the relevant financial reporting standards. Regular updates and fair value measurements ensure the swap remains an effective hedge and continues to align with the strategic financial objectives of the bond issuance (Das, 2006).

Ultimately, currency swaps offer project sponsors a powerful tool to lock in exchange rates, providing certainty and stability in the cash flows needed to service debt obligations. When employed strategically and managed effectively, currency swaps can shield bond-financed projects from the detrimental impacts of foreign exchange rate volatility.

Credit Default Swaps

In the realm of hedging strategies within bond financing, Credit Default Swaps (CDS) stand out as a critical instrument for risk mitigation, particularly against the potential default of an issuer. A Credit Default Swap is a form of derivative that resembles an insurance policy whereby the buyer of the CDS makes periodic payments to the seller, and in return, receives a payoff if the underlying financial instrument, typically a bond, defaults (Tett, 2009).

The functioning of Credit Default Swaps can be likened to an insurance contract, but it's vital to recognize that they are traded over-the-counter and their terms can be customized to fit the needs of the contracting parties. This flexibility allows for both standard hedging uses, where an investor might seek to protect their bond investments, and for speculation, where market participants might wish to bet on the creditworthiness of an issuer without holding the underlying bond (Stulz, 2010).

For project sponsors and capital market professionals, integrating CDS into their hedging strategy can serve as a safeguard against a project default. This not only provides protection but also may positively influence the project's bond ratings by reducing the perceived risk of default (Longstaff et al., 2005). Moreover, the presence of an active CDS market for a particular bond can offer deeper insights into the market's perception of credit risk, which can be informative for pricing and investor relations.

There are several nuances to consider when employing CDS in bond financing. First, the cost of a CDS, referred to as a spread, is measured in basis points per year over the notional amount of the bond being hedged. This cost reflects the market's assessment of how likely it is that the bond will default. Furthermore, if the creditworthiness of the bond issuer decreases, the spread widens, making the CDS more expensive and suggesting increased risk.

Despite their potential benefits, the use of Credit Default Swaps is not without controversy, as they can introduce counterparty risk—where the seller of the swap might itself default—and may contribute to systemic risk under certain market conditions (Duffie, 2010). Additionally, they require careful monitoring and management, as their value can fluctuate significantly with changing market conditions and credit ratings.

CDS can also influence the behaviour of bond issuers and holders in complex ways. For example, the existence of CDS contracts tied to specific bonds can create conflicting incentives for investors and could potentially exacerbate a financial crisis during periods of market stress (Brunnermeier & Oehmke, 2013). Therefore, capital market professionals must approach CDS with a critical understanding of these dynamics.

In summary, while Credit Default Swaps provide a mechanism to hedge credit risk in bond financing, their application demands skilled assessment and strategic use to ensure they contribute positively to a project's financial health. Their impact on the broader financial system further underscores the importance of regulatory oversight and prudent management in their use.

Chapter 18:
Repayment and Refinancing Options

Understanding the array of repayment and refinancing options is critical for professionals in project financing, specifically when these actions impact the returns and risks associated with bond issuances. This chapter delves into the mechanics and strategic considerations of bond repayment and refinancing options, providing insights into how they can be optimized within varying market conditions.

Call Provisions and Refinancing

Call provisions are clauses in bond contracts that allow the issuer to repay the bond before its maturity date. This can be a strategic tool under certain conditions, such as when interest rates have fallen since the bond was issued, presenting an opportunity to refinance at a lower rate. The decision to call a bond is influenced by factors like call premium costs, potential savings from reduced interest payments, and the current market rates (Fabozzi, 2012). When considering refinancing, project sponsors must weigh the benefits against the costs of transaction fees and any negative signalling to the market.

Sinking Funds and Debt Service Reserve Funds

Sinking funds and debt service reserve funds are mechanisms that serve as protection for both bondholders and issuers. A sinking fund is established by the issuer to repay part of the bond issue over time, preventing a large lump-sum payment at maturity. This can improve the bond's credit rating by reducing risk and demonstrates the issuer's commitment to meeting debt obligations (Kolb & Overdahl, 2010). Debt service reserve funds, on the other hand, act as a safety net for bondholders, ensuring that there are sufficient funds to cover future payments in times of cash flow uncertainty.

Refinancing Strategies in Volatile Markets

In volatile markets, well-timed refinancing can be a valuable strategy for project sponsors to manage their interest rate exposures and enhance project viability. Refinancing decisions must be informed by a careful analysis of interest rate forecasts, prepayment penalties, transaction costs, and the potential impacts on the project's cash flows (Fabozzi & Peterson Drake, 2019). When approached judiciously, refinancing can decrease costs and offer a more stable financial structure for the project's lifetime.

In conclusion, the formulation of repayment and refinancing strategies is a complex but vital element of bond issuance for project finance. It demands a precise understanding of market dynamics, contract terms, and the interplay of financial instruments. With these considerations in mind, professionals can craft approaches that mitigate risks, take advantage of favourable market conditions, and ultimately contribute to the success of the financed projects.

Call Provisions and Refinancing

Call provisions are critical components embedded in many bond contracts, granting the issuer the right, but not the obligation, to redeem a bond before its scheduled maturity date (Fabozzi, 2012). This feature provides issuers with the flexibility to adjust to changing market conditions, particularly in decreasing interest rate environments. Call options in bonds are strategic tools for issuers who anticipate a potential drop in interest rates, which could allow them to refinance existing debt at a lower cost. However, the inclusion of call provisions can also affect the appeal of bonds to investors, who face reinvestment risk should the bonds be called early.

Refinancing, on the other hand, refers to the replacement of an existing debt obligation with another debt obligation under different terms (Giddy, 2001). For project sponsors, this could entail issuing new bonds to repay older ones, typically to take advantage of lower prevailing interest rates, lengthen maturity, or alter the debt structure to better suit the project's cash flow patterns. Refinancing is a common practice in project finance as it can lead directly to interest expense savings and improved project viability.

When incorporating call provisions, issuers must evaluate the trade-offs between the added cost of these provisions—because investors generally demand a higher yield to compensate for early call risk—and the potential savings from refinancing. It is also crucial for issuers to assess the call premium, which is the additional sum above the face value of the bond that must be paid to investors upon a call (Hull, 2012). The timing of the call, the interest rate environment, and the future value of money all play potent roles in these calculations.

Call provisions and refinancing strategies are intrinsically connected to bond covenants and the legal framework governing the terms of issue. Issuers and their advisors must carefully navigate these arrangements to ensure that the bond structures align with the long-term financial strategy for the financed projects, all while maintaining compliance with market regulations and honouring investor expectations (Fabozzi et al., 2014).

Sinking Funds and Debt Service Reserve Funds

Understanding the mechanisms to ensure the repayment of bond debt is crucial for stakeholders in the project finance realm. Sinking funds and debt service reserve funds represent two pivotal components in this landscape. A sinking fund is a provision that necessitates the issuer to set aside funds periodically for retiring a portion of the debt before maturity. This practice aids in risk mitigation by reducing the debt load and reassuring investors about the issuer's commitment to repaying the principal (Fabozzi, 2018).

A sinking fund can be structured in several ways, including purchasing outstanding bonds in the open market or using the cash to call bonds at a predetermined price. By tempering the end-term debt burden, sinking funds introduce a degree of stability to the issuer's financial structure and can potentially enhance the credit rating of the bond issuance. It's important to note that the specific terms of a sinking fund, such as payment schedules and amounts, are typically defined in the bond indenture at issuance (Fabozzi, 2018).

Debt service reserve funds operate as a form of financial cushion, intended to cover interest and principal payments during periods of revenue shortfall. These reserves are commonly funded upfront through bond proceeds and serve as a safety net providing additional security to bondholders. The size of a debt service reserve fund typically correlates with the perceived risk profile of the project and the requirements stipulated by credit rating agencies or bond insurers (Schwartz & Aronson, 2020).

Both sinking funds and debt service reserve funds function as protective mechanisms that may also influence the bond's terms, including its interest rates and overall attractiveness to potential investors. As provisions that safeguard against default, they can also affect the structuring of senior and subordinate debt layers, intersecting with the broader strategies employed in managing cash flows and balancing the project's capital structure (Billington et al., 2019).

In conclusion, the incorporation of sinking funds and debt service reserve funds into the bond issuance framework reflects a proactive approach towards managing repayment obligations. These tools not only provide reassurance to investors but also temper the financial impact of debt on the issuer's balance sheet. Stakeholders in project finance must closely evaluate and structure these provisions to align them with the project's risk profile and ensure long-term financial stability and investor confidence.

Refinancing Strategies in Volatile Markets

Market volatility is an inevitable aspect of the financial world that significantly affects the strategy behind refinancing existing debt. Entities that have issued bonds as part of their project finance strategies must be adept at navigating this volatility to optimize their debt structures. Refinancing, in this context, involves replacing an outstanding bond issue with a new one, often with more favourable terms, matching the issuer's current financial position, market conditions, and future forecasts.

One critical strategy in volatile markets is the active monitoring of interest rate trends. Since interest rates significantly impact the cost of borrowing, understanding how these rates might change allows issuers to choose optimal refinancing points (Baker & Wurgler, 2006). By predicting periods of lower interest rates, sponsors can refinance at a reduced cost, thus decreasing the debt service obligations.

Another approach involves the use of derivatives and hedging techniques. For instance, interest rate swaps can be utilized where issuers exchange their existing risk profile for a more predictable one, thus mitigating the exposure to interest rate fluctuations (Smith et al., 1990). This strategy must be employed judiciously, as improper use can lead to increased risk and complexity.

Strategic use of call provisions within bond agreements allows issuers to retire debt before maturity during favourable market conditions. By including call options in their debt instruments, issuers retain the flexibility to seize refinancing opportunities when interest rates are beneficial (Fabozzi, 2007).

Amidst volatility, communication with investors and credit rating agencies becomes crucial. Maintaining transparency with stakeholders helps support the issuer's credit rating which can result in more favourable refinancing terms. It also prepares the investor base for potential changes in the debt structure (Fabozzi, 2007).

In summary, effective refinancing strategies in volatile markets require a proactive and informed approach to managing existing debt. Issuers must closely monitor market conditions, employ appropriate hedging strategies, make strategic use of call provisions, and maintain open lines of communication with relevant parties. By doing so, they can enhance their financial flexibility and potentially save significant costs over the long term. This proactive debt management is an integral skill for sponsors, bankers, and other financial professionals involved in project finance.

Chapter 19:
Environmental and Social Impact Assessments

In the realm of project finance, considerable importance is placed on the comprehensive evaluation of potential impacts that a project may have on the environment and society. The integration of Environmental and Social Impact Assessments (ESIAs) has become an intrinsic aspect of project planning and execution, ensuring that both risks and opportunities associated with environmental and social matters are thoroughly examined. This chapter delineates the process of incorporating Environmental, Social, and Governance (ESG) criteria into bonds, the steps involved in conducting impact assessments, and the subsequent reporting and compliance mandates.

Incorporating ESG Criteria in Bonds

Investors and other stakeholders are increasingly recognizing the significance of ESG criteria in project financing decisions, leading to the proliferation of sustainability-themed bonds, such as green, social, and sustainability bonds (Flammer, 2021). These bonds are designed with the intent to finance projects exhibiting positive environmental and social outcomes. Incorporating ESG criteria into bonds not only responds to market demand for responsible investment options but also can potentially enhance the bond issuer's reputation and reduce the cost of capital (Flammer, 2021).

The Impact Assessment Process

The assessment process often commences with a scoping exercise to identify potential environmental and social impacts, followed by the collection of baseline data. Subsequently, predictions and evaluations of likely impacts are made, and, where necessary, mitigation measures are proposed (Esteves et al., 2012). Assessments are typically carried out by interdisciplinary teams, including as a minimum, bank staff and external consultants, each bringing expertise in pertinent areas such as ecology, sociology, or health and safety.

For project sponsors, the assessment outcomes are not merely academic exercises; they inform project design adjustments, guide stakeholder engagement strategies, and help shape project management plans. Furthermore, these outcomes have a direct bearing on the project's acceptability to regulators, financial institutions, and the public at large (Esteves et al., 2012).

Reporting and Compliance

Ensuring adherence to ESG criteria is not a one-off task. Continuous reporting and compliance are crucial components of maintaining the credibility of ESG bonds post-issuance (Krosinsky & Purdom, 2019). Bond issuers are expected to provide periodic reports on the use of proceeds and the environmental and social outcomes of the projects they fund. Additionally, compliance procedures may involve regular audits and reviews by independent third parties to validate the reported outcomes against established benchmarks (Krosinsky & Purdom, 2019).

Through ongoing disclosure and engagement, issuers not only vindicate their commitments to ESG objectives but also safeguard the interests of investors, who expect transparency and accountability in the use of their funds. Thus, robust reporting frameworks serve as the linchpin for ensuring that ESG bonds stay true to their promise of delivering value while advancing sustainability and social wellbeing.

Incorporating ESG Criteria in Bonds

As stakeholders become increasingly conscientious about the environmental, social, and governance (ESG) impacts of their investments, incorporating ESG criteria into bonds has become a significant trend in the financial market. For project sponsors and capital market professionals, understanding the mechanics behind ESG criteria within the bond framework is crucial for aligning investments with these broader objectives.

ESG bonds typically encompass green, social, and sustainability bonds, each with specific criteria that must be met to ensure that funded projects achieve targeted outcomes (Gianfrate & Peri, 2019). Green bonds, for example, finance projects with environmental benefits, such as renewable energy developments or clean transportation. Social bonds focus on projects with positive social impacts, like affordable housing or accessible healthcare. Sustainability bonds combine elements of both, funding projects that have both environmental and social benefits.

To effectively incorporate ESG criteria into bonds, issuers must first establish a framework that defines the projects' eligibility criteria, the processes for project evaluation and selection, the management of proceeds, and a detailed reporting schedule (Flammer, 2021). The issuance process also includes obtaining a second-party opinion from an external reviewer, who will assess the bond's alignment with ESG principles based on established standards, such as the Green Bond Principles or Social Bond Principles sponsored by the International Capital Market Association (ICMA).

ESG bond issuances are further strengthened by ongoing reporting requirements, where issuers must regularly provide investors with updates on the projects' ESG performance and impacts. This reporting encourages transparency and enables investors to monitor the sustained commitment to the ESG criteria set forth at the issuance.

With bonds that incorporate ESG criteria, risk mitigation also takes on new dimensions. Investors are increasingly aware of the long-term risks associated with environmental and social issues, and consequently, ESG integration is seen as a way to reduce reputational, regulatory, and even credit risks (Krosinsky & Purdom, 2019). As a result, ESG bonds can potentially achieve more favourable interest rates and attract a more diverse investor base concerned with sustainable investing.

The integration of ESG criteria within bond financing is not just a trend but a reflection of a fundamental shift in the values that govern investment decisions. As environmental and social challenges become more pronounced, the ability for capital markets to direct funds towards sustainable projects becomes essential. Bankers, project sponsors, and financial professionals must therefore be well-versed in ESG principles and the structuring of ESG bonds to meet the evolving demands of investors and society at large.

The Impact Assessment Process

The process of assessing environmental and social impacts is a cornerstone of sustainable project finance, frequently tied to the issuance of ESG bonds. This section delineates the structured framework and methodologies used to conduct a comprehensive Impact Assessment (IA) that informs project sponsors, financial institutions, and other stakeholders.

The IA process typically starts with the screening stage, during which projects are categorized based on their potential impacts. The significance and scale of these impacts determine the level and depth of assessment required (International Association for Impact Assessment,

2015). After screening, the process transitions to the scoping phase. Here, the key issues are identified and a plan is created, specifying the assessment's scope and laying out the methodologies to be used for examining the anticipated impacts.

Data collection and analysis form the core of the impact assessment. Researchers engage various quantitative and qualitative methods to gather information on the baseline conditions and to predict future scenarios with the project in place (Therivel & Wood, 2017). Impact prediction tools range from simple checklists to complex modelling software, chosen based on the specific context and requirements of the project.

Once the potential impacts are understood, the assessment moves into mitigation and management planning. Effective strategies are developed to minimize, mitigate, or compensate for the adverse impacts, while enhancing positive outcomes. The next stage involves the preparation of the Environmental and Social Impact Assessment (ESIA) report, which details the findings and recommendations, serving as a vehicle for decision-making and for informing stakeholders.

Public consultation and disclosure are imperative components throughout the IA process. Garnering feedback from affected communities and stakeholders ensures transparency, incorporates local knowledge into the assessment, and fosters public acceptance (United Nations Environment Programme, 2018).

Finally, the process doesn't conclude after the report is submitted. Monitoring and follow-up are crucial post-assessment activities that validate the effectiveness of the mitigation measures and ensure compliance with the environmental and social management plans proposed in the ESIA report.

In summary, the impact assessment process is a systematic approach that integrates environmental and social considerations into project finance. Its ultimate goal is to promote sustainable development, satisfy regulatory requirements, and support the successful issuance and management of ESG bonds.

Reporting and Compliance

The institutionalization of Environmental and Social Impact Assessments (ESIAs) within project finance is not merely about conducting due diligence or securing financing; it equally involves a profound commitment to ongoing compliance and transparent reporting. For stakeholders including bankers, project sponsors, and insurance professionals, who operate within the realm of bonds as financial instruments, the convergence of compliance requirements and the reporting protocol is particularly acute under the purview of ESG-centered bonds.

In accordance with international best practices and regulatory standards, such as the Equator Principles (Equator Principles Association) and the guidelines established by the International Finance Corporation (IFC, 2012), reporting and compliance necessitate rigorous documentation and periodic disclosure of environmental and social performance. Such frameworks underscore the importance of developing a robust Environmental and Social Management System (ESMS) that delineates clear procedures for monitoring, reporting, and correcting non-compliance throughout the lifecycle of a project.

Precisely, within the post-issuance phase of bond financing, sponsors must adhere to covenants that include environmental and social clauses obligating them to carry out regular assessments against the initially stated objectives and to publish the findings in accordance with agreed schedules. Depending on the type of bond, this could manifest as annual ESG reports for green bonds, updates on social impacts for social bonds, or comprehensive sustainability reports for sustainability bonds.

Compliance also interacts intimately with the rating of such bonds. As assessors like Moody's or Standard & Poor's increasingly integrate ESG risk into their credit assessments, non-compliance can result in rating downgrades, impacting refinancing options and market perceptions of creditworthiness (Krosinsky & Purdom, 2021).

It is pertinent for professionals entwined in the bond issuance process to stay abreast of emission standards, labour laws, and community engagement policies in relation to the target markets of the issued bonds. For transgressions or failures identified during reporting, mechanisms must be in place for remediation and mitigation. In severe cases, non-compliance could lead to legal consequences, bond covenant breaches, or even the triggering of early redemption clauses.

Ultimately, the ethos behind reporting and compliance in the context of ESG-focused financial instruments is not merely an obligatory exercise; it serves as a barometer of transparency and responsiveness towards environmental and social imperatives. It is this accountability that not only sustains investor confidence but also buttresses the integrity of the bond itself as a tool for sustainable development.

Chapter 20:
Tax Considerations in Bond Issuance

Tax implications play a pivotal role in bond issuances and can significantly influence the cost of capital for issuers, as well as the after-tax yield for investors. Project sponsors and financial professionals must thoroughly comprehend the tax aspects of bond financing to optimize the structure and appeal of their offerings. This chapter addresses key tax considerations that impact the issuance process.

Tax-Exempt Bonds

For certain types of bond issuances, notably municipal bonds, the interest income received by investors is often exempt from federal income taxes, and sometimes state and local taxes as well (Moody's Investors Service, 2021). This tax advantage can allow municipalities and qualifying issuers to finance projects at a lower interest cost compared to taxable bonds. However, tax-exempt bonds must comply with strict requirements set out by the Internal Revenue Service (IRS) regarding their use and the purposes for which they finance. The arbitrage rules, for instance, limit the ability of issuers to earn profits from investing bond proceeds in higher-yielding investments.

Taxable Bonds

Most corporate bonds and other types of project finance bonds fall under the taxable category, meaning that the investors' interest income is subject to federal and possibly state and local income taxation.

Despite this taxation, taxable bonds provide the issuer with the flexibility to fund projects that may not qualify for tax-exempt financing. In recent years, the issuance of taxable municipal bonds has increased as these bonds provide issuers access to a broader investor base, including those not seeking tax-exempt income (Feldstein & Fabozzi, 2021).

Cross-Border Tax Implications

Bond issuances that attract international investors or that are issued by entities in different countries can add another layer of complexity to tax considerations. Cross-border taxation issues such as withholding taxes, tax treaties, and differences in tax regimes can affect both issuers and investors. Issuers must be careful to structure their bond offerings in a manner that is tax-efficient for investors in varying jurisdictions, taking into account bilateral tax treaties that may provide for reduced withholding tax rates or exemptions (PwC, 2020).

Understanding these tax implications is crucial for structuring financially viable bond deals that minimize tax liabilities and maximize net proceeds for the project. Project sponsors, bankers, and capital market professionals must incorporate tax planning into their overall strategic finance plan to ensure that the structure of their bond offering meets the needs of their project while also being attractive to potential investors. Consultation with tax attorneys and advisors with expertise in bond financing is typically an integral part of this process.

Tax-Exempt Bonds

Within the sphere of bond issuance, tax-exempt bonds represent a critical financing tool for various types of infrastructure and public projects. Understanding the benefits and limitations of tax-exempt bonds is essential for capital market professionals, project sponsors, and others involved in project finance. These bonds, typically issued by state or local governments, afford investors the advantage of not having to pay federal income tax on the interest earned (Internal Revenue Service, n.d.). In certain cases, state and local tax exemptions may also apply, further increasing the attractiveness of these bonds to investors.

The tax-exempt status of these bonds can often translate into lower interest costs for the issuer compared to taxable bonds, because investors are willing to accept a lower yield due to the tax benefits (U.S. Securities and Exchange Commission, 2017). This makes tax-exempt bonds a cost-effective borrowing option for qualifying projects, including transportation infrastructure, schools, hospitals, and affordable housing, among others. When issuing tax-exempt bonds, it is vital for issuers to comply with various Internal Revenue Service (IRS) rules and regulations to maintain the bonds' tax-exempt status.

Private activity bonds (PABs) are a category of tax-exempt bonds that can also be utilized under certain conditions for projects with a qualified public benefit that are led by private entities (U.S. Department of the Treasury, n.d.). However, PABs are subject to additional rules, restrictions, and volume caps set by the IRS to qualify for tax-exempt status.

When considering the use of tax-exempt bonds, it is important to factor in the arbitrage restrictions that limit the ability of issuers to benefit disproportionately from borrowing at tax-exempt rates while investing in higher-yielding taxable securities (Internal Revenue Service, n.d.). Additionally, certain post-issuance compliance requirements must be met to retain the tax-exempt status of the bonds, including the use of proceeds and timely reporting.

For project sponsors and those structuring bond deals, understanding the interplay between tax-exemption and project eligibility, financing terms, and compliance requirements is crucial. The appropriate structuring of tax-exempt bonds can result in substantial cost savings, making projects financially viable and attractive to investors. In comparison to their taxable counterparts, tax-exempt bonds require careful alignment with IRS regulations to ensure that all tax benefits are fully realized.

Taxable Bonds

In the realm of bond issuance, understanding the distinctions and the intricate fiscal implications of taxable bonds is crucial for project sponsors and financing professionals. Taxable bonds, unlike their tax-exempt counterparts, generate interest income that is subject to federal and, in many cases, state and local income taxes. These bonds are often issued by corporations, but can also be issued by municipalities when the funds are purposed for activities that do not provide a significant benefit to the public (Internal Revenue Service, 2021).

Taxable bonds typically offer higher yields to compensate investors for the additional tax burden. This inherently marks a fundamental trade-off in the bond market: the higher interest income attracts investors seeking more lucrative returns, albeit aligned with a higher tax liability (Fabozzi, 2015). From a project sponsor's perspective, this can inform strategic decisions on whether the higher interest costs associated with taxable bonds are justified by the project's return on investment and financial objectives.

Furthermore, certain federal programs may offer taxable bonds with credit subsidies or direct payments to issuers to encourage investment in specific areas, such as energy projects or economic recovery initiatives. The Build America Bonds (BABs), introduced under the American Recovery and Reinvestment Act of 2009, are a prime example, where the Treasury Department provided a subsidy to issuers of certain qualified taxable bonds (U.S. Department of the Treasury, 2009).

When considering the issuance of taxable bonds, the issuer must meticulously calculate the taxable equivalent yield—a critical concept that denotes the pretax yield that a tax-exempt bond would need to possess to be equivalent to the yield of a taxable bond. This calculation guides investors in comparing the potential benefits across different tax treatments and investment considerations (Fabozzi, 2015).

In a rapidly evolving bond market, it's noteworthy that taxable bonds are not constrained by the same exhaustive regulations that govern tax-exempt bonds. This can afford issuers and their counsel greater flexibility in how the bond proceeds can be utilized, an aspect that bears significant weight in structuring deals for project financing.

Ultimately, taxable bonds play an essential role in a diverse array of financing strategies. By meticulously weighing tax obligations against projected financial outcomes, bankers and project sponsors can avoid onerous tax consequences while optimizing their investment portfolio or project funding structure to ensure a successful venture.

Cross-Border Tax Implications

When sponsoring projects through bond issuances that involve cross-border elements, sponsors and their advisors must navigate a complex web of international tax laws and treaties. This section delves into the multifaceted tax implications that arise when bonds are issued across jurisdictions.

One of the most prominent considerations in such transactions is the tax treatment of interest payments. Different countries have unique rules governing taxation on interest income. For instance, the United States generally imposes a 30% withholding tax on interest paid to foreign bondholders, which can be reduced or eliminated if a tax treaty exists between the involved countries (IRS, 2022). These treaties are crucial to understand as they can significantly affect the net return for investors and the cost of capital for issuers.

Moreover, when bonds are issued in a foreign currency, issuers must also consider the tax consequences of foreign exchange gains or losses. The treatment of these can vary wildly, with some jurisdictions classifying them as ordinary income or capital gains, and others providing specific hedging rules (Jorisch, 2019).

Transfer pricing is another tax issue of cross-border bond issuance. Multinational companies must price their intercompany debt in a manner that aligns with the arm's length principle, meaning that the interest rates and terms should be comparable to what would be charged between independent parties (OECD, 2017). Compliance with transfer pricing guidelines is critical to prevent punitive tax adjustments and penalties.

A lack of alignment in tax regulations across countries can also lead to double taxation on the same income, or in some cases, double non-taxation. This concern becomes prominent as bond issuances often involve multiple jurisdictions. To mitigate such scenarios, it is essential to utilize the provisions of double tax treaties where possible, allowing for relief through tax credits or exemptions (Davies et al., 2020).

Lastly, the potential for tax law changes must also be considered. Since tax policies can significantly impact the desirability of bonds, shifts in legislation could affect not only future bond issuances but also the tax position on existing instruments. Keeping updated with international tax policy developments is therefore vital for all parties engaged in cross-border bond markets.

Chapter 21:
Defaults and Remedies

In the preceding chapters, we have meticulously navigated the intricacies of bond issuances, structures, and associated strategies in project finance. It's now crucial to discuss the implications and remedial measures pertaining to defaults in bonds. Understanding how defaults are managed is of paramount importance for bankers, project sponsors, insurance professionals, and capital market stakeholders.

Events of Default and Responses

Default is a significant failure to adhere to the terms of a bond. The implications of default are extensive, affecting not just the financial standing of the project but also the market's perception of the involved entities. Events that can trigger a default may include missed payments, violation of covenants, or insolvency. Once an event of default occurs, the trustee, or in some cases the bondholders, must respond in alignment with the agreed-upon terms of the bond indenture. This response often takes the form of accelerated repayment demands, legal action, or starting the process of restructuring the debt (Fabozzi, 2018).

Restructuring of Debt

Restructuring of debt is a process embarked upon to alter the terms of the bond, with an intent to improve the issuer's ability to service the debt. This may involve changes to the interest rate, extension of maturity dates, or a reduction in the principal amount owed (Altman

& Hotchkiss, 2006). It serves as an instrumental tool for ailing projects to regain stability while providing bondholders with an opportunity to salvage value that would otherwise be lost in a total default.

Recourse and Non-Recourse Bonds

The distinction between recourse and non-recourse bonds becomes most evident during default episodes. With recourse bonds, bondholders have the legal right to seize the issuer's assets beyond the collateral specified if the issuer fails to make the required payments. In contrast, non-recourse bonds limit bondholders' claims to the collateral pledged, shielding the issuer's other assets. This limitation represents a higher risk for investors and hence impacts the bond's credit rating and terms (Fabozzi, 2018).

In summary, a comprehensive understanding of defaults and remedies in bond issuances is essential for industry professionals. It allows for better risk mitigation and provides a roadmap for navigating the complications that arise when a project encounters financial distress.

Events of Default and Responses

Considered a critical component within the framework of bond financings, the events of default and corresponding responses delineate the threshold where actions may be precipitated by the breach of bond covenants or other contractual obligations. An event of default is a specific, predefined condition or set of circumstances that, upon occurrence, gives rise to the rights of bondholders or trustees to demand remedial action, up to and including the acceleration of debt repayment (Fabozzi, 2018).

Within the context of project finance, certain events of default are commonly observed. These include, but are not limited to, the failure to make principal or interest payments, breaches of covenants, warranties or representations, insolvency or bankruptcy proceedings, and in some instances, adverse changes in the project's economic viability or the political landscape that could materially affect the project's capacity to meet its obligations (Esty, 2014).

Responses to such events are varied and must be executed in accordance with the bond indenture. Upon an event of default, a trustee typically liaises with bondholders to discuss potential courses of action. These actions may range from waiving the default, restructuring the terms of the bond, or exercising the rights to accelerate the debt. The trustee also has the right, but not the obligation, to take legal action against the project sponsor on behalf of the bondholders (Fabozzi, 2018).

Importantly, the definition of an event of default, along with the associated remedies, must be clearly articulated in the bond documentation to ensure that all parties are aware of the triggers and possible solutions. The remedies provided to bondholders upon default are typically enforced by the trustee, who acts in their interest. Available remedies for bondholders may include demanding immediate payment in full or seizing any collateral pledged against the debt (Smith & Warner, 1979).

Moreover, bondholders may choose to restructure the debt, a process that often necessitates negotiations concerning amendments to the payment schedule, interest rates, or maturity dates. This response balances the immediate need for bondholder protection with the long-term viability of the project and the potential for future recovery (Esty, 2014).

In summary, the 'Events of Default and Responses' section outlines the contractual mechanisms by which bondholders may seek recourse in instances where the issuer has faltered on its obligations. It serves as both a deterrent against the issuer's noncompliance and a structured path forward in the event such compliance falters, thereby stabilizing the bond issuance ecosystem and enforcing the bond covenant framework.

Restructuring of Debt

When a bond issuer faces financial difficulties that hamper its ability to meet debt obligations, debt restructuring presents a remedial strategy that can avoid the dire implications of defaulting. For all stakeholders involved - from project sponsors and bankers to insurance and capital market professionals - understanding the intricacies of debt restructuring is crucial for managing the eventuality of distressed bonds within the scope of project finance. Restructuring of debt typically refers to the modification of the existing terms of a bond issuance to provide the issuer with an opportunity to regain financial stability and maintain business operations (Fabozzi et al., 2018).

One of the primary steps in restructuring debt involves renegotiation of the bond terms with the bondholders. This may include adjusting the coupon rates, extending the maturity dates, reducing the face value of the bonds, or offering equity in lieu of debt (Moyer, 2021). In complex scenarios, this process may require the establishment of a creditors' committee to negotiate and accept the terms on behalf of all bondholders. The goal here is to realign the repayment schedule to the issuer's forecasted cash flows, ensuring that the project that initially necessitated the bond issuance remains viable.

During restructuring, safeguarding the interests of both the bondholders and the issuer is paramount. The issuer seeks to diminish the debt burden and avoid the far-reaching consequences of bankruptcy, while bondholders aim to recover the maximum amount of their investment rather than facing the risks associated with liquidation. The process is underpinned by the principle that renegotiated terms are more favourable than the outcomes following a default. Despite the inherent complexities, a successful restructuring can bolster the issuer's financial health while preserving the bondholders' investment, potentially leading to an acceptable resolution for all parties involved (Altman & Hotchkiss, 2006).

Debt restructuring for distressed bonds may also occur within the context of a formal bankruptcy process, in which the bond's terms are modified according to a reorganization plan approved by the court. However, if managed out-of-court, the process can be less costly and preserve more value for both the issuer and the bondholders (Gilson, 2017). Professionals in the field must understand legal and regulatory implications as well as market sentiments which invariably shape restructuring negotiations.

In sum, the section on "Restructuring of Debt" delves into the strategies, negotiations, and mechanisms behind altering the conditions of bond agreements to mitigate the financial stress on the issuer and provide an adequate recovery path for investors. The ability to skilfully navigate the restructuring process is an invaluable skill for those involved in project finance, where the stakes are notably high, and the margin for error is notably slim.

Recourse and Non-Recourse Bonds

When a bond defaults, the nature of the bond dictates the extent to which investors can claim assets or revenue streams to recover their investments. This delineation is primarily defined in terms of recourse and non-recourse bonds, critical constructs in the event of a default. Understanding the differences between these two types of bonds is essential for project sponsors, bankers, and all practitioners involved in the structuring and analysis of project finance bond issues.

Recourse bonds provide bondholders with the right to claim not just the project's assets but also additional assets of the issuer in the event the project fails to generate the expected revenues to service the bond's debt obligations. This gives lenders a higher level of security, as they have a claim to a broader asset pool. In the context of project finance, recourse bonds can persuade investors to participate in financing, knowing that there is a safety net beyond the project's earnings. Yet, this increased security comes at the cost of potentially higher liability for the issuer, which can impact the issuer's balance sheet and credit rating (Fabozzi, 2015).

Non-recourse bonds, conversely, limit investor claims solely to the earnings and assets of the project being financed. These types of bonds are generally used in project finance when the sponsoring entity wishes to isolate project risk from its assets and preserve its creditworthiness for future endeavours (Esty, 2004). Non-recourse financing is attractive for projects where the risk profile is higher, as it protects the sponsors' assets beyond the project. However, the trade-off is typically a higher interest rate to compensate bondholders for the additional risk associated with the limited recourse (Yescombe, 2014).

In the occurrence of a default, bondholders in non-recourse arrangements typically have limited options and might need to take control of the project to mitigate losses. This process can be complex and time-consuming, as it often requires operating expertise outside of the bondholders' core competencies. In contrast, recourse bonds afford greater flexibility in recovery efforts post-default. Notwithstanding, both options require careful legal structuring to ensure the rights and obligations of all parties are clear from the outset.

Considering the ramifications of issuing recourse versus non-recourse bonds in project finance, it's essential to weigh the legal, financial, and operational implications. The choice impacts the project's cost of capital, risk distribution, and the sponsors' long-term financial health.

Chapter 22:
The Role of Insurance in Bond Financing

In our previous discussions, we have navigated through the complexities and rigors of bond financing, scrutinizing everything from the inception of project bonds to the labyrinth of regulations that govern their issuance and management. In this chapter, we shift our focus to a critical adjunct in the realm of bond financing, the insurance industry, and its profound impact on the marketability and creditworthiness of bond issuances.

Enhancing Creditworthiness with Insurance

When it comes to bond financing, the concept of creditworthiness reigns supreme. Investors are constantly on the lookout for indicators of security and reliability, thus influencing their decision-making process. Insurance plays a pivotal role in this context by providing a safety net that can enhance the perceived credit quality of bond issuances. One common form of this is bond insurance, where an insurance company guarantees the repayment of principal and interest to bondholders in the event the issuer defaults (Schwarcz, 2002).

The incorporation of insurance into bond financing can translate into higher credit ratings, lowering the cost of capital for issuers. Such credit enhancements can be particularly impactful for smaller or lesser-known entities that might otherwise struggle to attract investors (Fabozzi, 2015). Furthermore, insurance can mitigate specific project risks related to construction, operations, or revenue streams, thus providing a more stable investment vehicle.

Bond Insurance Products

Within the scope of bond insurance, there are several products tailored to address various risks associated with bond financing. Wrap policies are a form of insurance that 'wraps' around the bond, ensuring the timely payment of interest and principal. Further, dedicated policies might address construction risk, operational risk, or even catastrophic events.

Default insurance, another critical product, offers protection against issuer defaults. Surety bonds, on the other hand, provide a promise by a third party – the surety – to cover the issuer's obligations if they cannot meet them. Additionally, credit enhancement products, which can take numerous forms including letters of credit or liquidity facilities, are instrumental in reinforcing investor confidence by guaranteeing additional liquidity or credit support (Fabozzi, 2015).

Case Studies: Insured Bonds in Action

Let's consider a real-life application of insurance in bond financing through various case studies. A paradigmatic example is the use of insurance in municipal bond issuances. Municipalities often rely on insurance to obtain better interest rates than their standalone credit profiles might command (Benson et al., 2004). By paying a premium for insurance, they effectively buy a higher credit rating, which in turn reduces borrowing costs.

Another case study is infrastructure projects, where insurance mechanisms have been utilized to secure long-term financing. For instance, wrap insurance has been used to assure the completion and operational viability of toll roads, bridges, and tunnels, ensuring that revenue disruption risks are covered, and investor concerns are assuaged.

These case studies underscore the transformational impact that insurance can have on bond financing, enabling projects that may not have been feasible or attractive to investors to gain the necessary capital support.

In conclusion, insurance in bond financing serves as a cornerstone of risk mitigation, elevating projects' creditworthiness and unlocking access to capital. As we delve deeper into the intricacies of bond financing, the alliance between insurance elements and bond issuances becomes increasingly strategic, offering a path to resilience and confidence in investment decisions within this sophisticated financial landscape.

Enhancing Creditworthiness with Insurance

Within the realm of bond financing, the enhancement of creditworthiness is a pivotal concern for issuers aiming to secure optimal terms and rates. Insurance products play a critical role in strengthening the appeal of a bond offering by providing a level of security to investors and decreasing the inherent risks associated with repayment (Schwarcz, 2002). When issuing bonds for project financing, sponsors seek mechanisms that assure investors of timely interest and principal payments, thereby achieving a favourable assessment from rating agencies and a reduction in the cost of capital.

Insurance policies, when underwritten specifically for bond issues, can significantly elevate an issuer's credit rating. This is achieved by transferring the default risk from the bond issuer to the insurer. In other words, should the issuer become unable to meet debt obligations, the insurer is contractually obligated to cover the payments, which lessens the perceived risk and in turn, can lead to a higher bond rating (Monk, 2009).

The mechanisms through which insurance enhances creditworthiness include bond insurance, also known as a financial guarantee, and letters of credit provided by banking institutions. These instruments offer distinct advantages: bond insurance typically covers the life of the bond and ensures that investors receive timely payments, while a letter of credit often serves to facilitate short-term liquidity. The creditworthiness of the insurance provider itself is paramount, for it underpins the validity of the guarantee. Therefore, insurers with high credit ratings are indispensable in this scenario, as their backing is viewed as a substantial endorsement of the bond's reliability.

Insurers also conduct their own thorough due diligence before underwriting bonds. This process can uncover potential risks not initially identified by the bond issuer or other involved parties. By insisting on corrective measures or covenant adjustments, insurers can enforce stronger risk management and enhance the overall financial health of the bond issue (Merna & Al-Thani, 2008).

However, it's essential to recognize that insurance is not a panacea for all risks associated with bonds. The increase in transaction costs due to insurance premiums must be balanced against the potential benefits of obtaining a better rating and lower interest rates. The decision to utilize insurance as a credit enhancement tool must involve a rigorous analysis of the project's specific risks and the market conditions under which the bond is issued. Nevertheless, a nuanced understanding of the role of insurance in augmenting creditworthiness can yield substantial benefits for issuers within the bond financing framework.

Bond Insurance Products

In the context of bond financing, insurance products serve as a critical tool for reducing the credit risk associated with bond issuances and enhancing the appeal of bonds to potential investors. Bond insurance, also known as a financial guarantee, is a policy taken out by a bond issuer that promises to cover the principal and interest payments to bondholders in the event of a default. This section delves into the function and utility of bond insurance products in the realm of project finance.

Bond insurance offers investors confidence in the creditworthiness of their investment and can often lead to an increase in the bond's rating. This uplift in rating typically results in reduced borrowing costs for the issuer due to the perceived lower risk of default (Fabozzi, 2018). Bond insurers assess the issuer's credit strength and project viability before underwriting the insurance policy and may require enhancement measures to mitigate risks.

The principal insurance products in this arena include municipal bond insurance, corporate bond insurance, and collateralized debt obligation (CDO) guarantees. Municipal bond insurance is predominantly utilized for bonds issued by local governments and their agencies, whereas corporate bond insurance is applicable to enterprises seeking to finance their activities. CDO guarantees are related to pools of debt obligations that have been packaged together, providing insurance for this category of financial instruments.

The method of obtaining bond insurance involves both quantitative and qualitative analysis of the bond issuer, the project's fundamentals, and the overall market conditions. Bond insurers will often require detailed financial models and projections, as well as stringent adherence to specific terms and covenants that align with industry best practices and regulatory requirements (McKinsey & Company, 2009).

Critics have noted that while bond insurance can decrease financing costs and boost investor confidence, it can also introduce counterparty risk if the insurer itself faces financial difficulties. The 2008 financial crisis underscored the need for due diligence on the part of both the issuers and the investors and has led to more stringent underwriting standards within the industry (Bloomberg, 2009).

Moreover, the market for bond insurance has seen changes post-crisis, with fewer insurers in the market and a reduced percentage of bonds being insured. Nevertheless, bond insurance remains a crucial instrument, especially for smaller or less well-known issuers seeking access to capital at more favourable terms.

In summary, bond insurance is a product that enhances the marketability of bonds by mitigating the risk of default through the backing of an insurance company, thus contributing to lower interest rates and a potentially higher rating. The decision to insure a bond will weigh the benefits of improved credit against the cost of the insurance premium.

References:

Fabozzi, F. J. (2018). Handbook of Fixed Income Securities. Wiley.

McKinsey & Company. (2009). The use of financial guarantee insurance in project finance. Infrastructure Finance Review.

Bloomberg. (2009). Financial Guarantors After the Crisis. Bloomberg Markets.

Case Studies: Insured Bonds in Action

Insured bonds represent a strategic financial mechanism utilized to lower the risk to investors and enhance the creditworthiness of bond offerings. An additional layer of assurance is infused into the bond through an insurance policy, safeguarding bondholders against default (Kroll, 2018). Insurance can be an indispensable tool in constructing stabilized project finance structures. This section explores real-world applications that demonstrate the nuanced empowerment that insurance provides in bond financing.

The Big Dig: The Central Artery/Tunnel Project, commonly known as the Big Dig, stands as a quintessential example showcasing the utilization of insured bonds. Based in Boston, the project aimed at alleviating congestion, yet was marked by high costs and risks. To finance this large-scale infrastructure, a mix of bonds was issued, including some with insurance. This insurance mitigated the risks associated with the long-term nature and complexity of the project, thus attracted a broader base of investors and achieved a lower interest rate complacency (Fabozzi et al., 2008). The bond insurance assured the investors of a timely interest and principal payment, contributing to the project's eventual successful completion.

Hurricane Catastrophe Funds: In the wake of devastating hurricanes, certain U.S. states, such as Florida, have instituted catastrophe funds. These funds, financed through the issuance of insured bonds, allow for immediate access to capital post-disaster for rebuilding efforts. The insurance component of these bonds alleviates the apprehension of potential investors regarding the uncertainty of payback due to the bonds being reliant on future catastrophe events (Cummins & Sessions, 2007). The insurance therefore not only backstops the bonds but also provides a pool of funds ready for emergency response.

Social Housing Ventures: Social housing projects often use insured bonds to finance the development or refurbishment of affordable housing units. A case in point is New York City's social housing, where bond insurance played a critical role in managing investors' concerns about potential defaults owing to the fluctuating real estate markets and varied tenant demographics. Insurance improved the bond rating, lowered the interest rates, and provided a safety net for investors while aiding the city in its goal to create or preserve affordable housing for low-income residents.

These case studies illustrate the value-added by insurance in bond financing, reducing perceived risk by investors and allowing project sponsors to fund projects with better terms. Bond insurance proves to be a decisive factor in the completion and success of projects across different sectors, enhancing the attractiveness of bond issuances to a wider array of investors.

Chapter 23:
The Evolution of Digital Bonds

As we edge further into a technologically dominated era, the financial landscape continues to evolve, embracing digital transformation in every aspect, including bonds—a crucial tool in project financing. Digital bonds, or bonds issued and managed through blockchain and other digital platforms, represent not just innovation but a potential paradigm shift in how project sponsors and capital market professionals approach bond issuances. This chapter delves into the technological advancements that shape digital bonds and their implications for risk mitigation, efficiency, and accessibility within the bond market.

Blockchain-Enabled Bonds

Blockchain technology's irrefutable ledger system has laid down the backbone for digital bonds, providing an unprecedented level of security and transparency in bond transactions. By utilizing blockchain, issuers can streamline the bond issuance process, reduce the incidence of fraud, and enhance the traceability of bond ownership (Tapscott & Tapscott, 2016). Moreover, the innate structure of distributed ledger technology ensures that bond covenants and post-issuance obligations are coded into the bond itself, further mitigating legal and regulatory risks associated with conventional bond issuances.

Smart contracts, an intrinsic feature of blockchain platforms, automate bond payments and other contractual obligations, which drastically reduces the possibility of human error and enforces adherence to the bond's terms (Szabo, 1997). The automation of these processes decreases administrative costs and time delays, paving the way for a more efficient bond market and potentially transforming risk profiles associated with bond issuances (Casey & Vigna, 2018).

Digital Platforms for Bond Issuance

The evolution of digital bonds is also characterized by the development and adoption of digital platforms designed specifically for bond issuance and trading. These platforms offer project sponsors and investors a streamlined process for bond issuance, from origination to settlement. Through digital platforms, the marketing and sale of bonds can tap into a broader investment base, especially by reaching out to retail investors who otherwise may not have direct access to traditional bond markets. Additionally, these platforms support real-time tracking of bond performance, facilitating immediate risk assessment and enhancing liquidity in the bond market.

In summary, digital bonds mark a significant milestone in the financial sector's journey towards a more transparent, efficient, and inclusive market. While there are challenges to widespread adoption—such as regulatory adaptation and integration with existing financial systems—the future of digital bonds is poised to redefine project finance. As market participants become more familiar with the mechanics of blockchain and digital platforms, we can expect to see a significant increase in the number of digital bonds and an overall transformation of the bond issuance process.

Blockchain-Enabled Bonds

The integration of blockchain technology into the bond market represents a significant evolution in the digitalization of financial instruments. In the context of project finance, blockchain-enabled bonds, also known as smart bonds or distributed ledger bonds, offer a new frontier in the issuance, management, and trading of debt securities. These instruments embody a transformative approach by leveraging the inherent features of blockchain technology—transparency, security, and efficiency—to optimize the lifecycle of a bond from issuance to maturity (Tapscott & Tapscott, 2016).

Blockchain-enabled bonds are issued and managed on a blockchain platform, which allows for an immutable and chronological ledger of transactions, making every phase of the bond's lifecycle trackable and tamper-proof. The potential benefits to stakeholders in the bond issuance ecosystem are manifold. For issuers, blockchain can streamline the cumbersome and often costly process of bond issuance by reducing the need for intermediaries, thus potentially lowering issuance costs and improving access to capital. Investors benefit from greater transparency and real-time visibility into bond performance and ownership, which can enhance liquidity and market confidence (Antoniou, Paudyal, & Viola, 2021).

One illustrative example of a blockchain-enabled bond is the 'bond-i,' launched by the World Bank in 2018. The bond-i, short for Blockchain Operated New Debt Instrument, was the world's first bond to be created, allocated, transferred, and managed through its lifecycle using blockchain technology (World Bank, 2018). The issuance demonstrated the feasibility and interest in blockchain-based bonds as a method to reduce operational complexity and costs while increasing efficiency and transparency.

The practical application of blockchain in bond financing includes the use of smart contracts—self-executing contracts with the terms of the agreement directly written into code—which can automate interest payments and other covenants based on predetermined rules. These capabilities can mitigate administrative burdens and the risk of human error, while also streamlining compliance and legal enforcement. Additionally, blockchain's inherent security features can strengthen the bond markets against fraud and default risks, a crucial consideration for risk mitigation strategies in project finance.

Despite the promising benefits, the widespread adoption of blockchain-enabled bonds faces challenges. Regulatory uncertainty, the need for technological infrastructure development, and questions regarding interoperability with traditional financial systems are often cited as hurdles (Antoniou et al., 2021). Moreover, transitioning to blockchain-based systems requires significant investment in technology and training, presenting an adoption barrier for some market participants.

As project sponsors, bankers, and other capital market professionals continue to seek methods to finance projects efficiently and securely, blockchain-enabled bonds offer an innovative mechanism that aligns with these goals. By understanding the intricacies of blockchain applications in the bonding process, stakeholders can be better positioned to leverage digital bonds' potential to enhance project finance outcomes.

Digital Platforms for Bond Issuance

As the financial sector continues to be transformed by the advent of digital technologies, the process of bond issuance has also begun to evolve. Digital platforms for bond issuance represent a significant shift in the infrastructure and methodology used by many in the capital markets, including bankers, project sponsors, and insurance professionals. The objective of these platforms is to streamline the issuance process, reduce costs, increase efficiency, and facilitate access to the markets—thereby democratizing the opportunities in project financing.

Digital bond issuance platforms operate by leveraging technology to automate many of the steps which traditionally required manual intervention and presented potential bottlenecks. These platforms incorporate various features such as document management, compliance checks, and communication tools—all integrated into one system. This approach not only accelerates the bond issuance process but also enhances transparency and accuracy by minimizing the risk of human error (Scott et al., 2020).

One of the standout features of digital bond issuance platforms is their use of distributed ledger technology, particularly blockchain. Blockchain is the underlying technology behind these platforms, which facilitates immutable record-keeping and instant sharing of information across a network of authorized participants (Gomber et al., 2018). This ensures that all parties have access to the same information in real-time, thereby improving the trust and verification processes throughout a bond's lifecycle.

Fintech companies have developed platforms that offer end-to-end solutions for bond issuances. From the initial documentation process to the final allocation and settlement, these platforms can cover the entire spectrum of activities, even integrating digital wallets for receipt of investment and subsequent disbursement of funds. By using smart contracts, digital bond issuance platforms can automate the execution of complex terms and conditions related to bond servicing, such as coupon payments and maturity settlements (Mills et al., 2019).

In addition to improving the mechanical aspects of bond issuance, digital platforms have also made a marked impact on the engagement with investors. These platforms frequently include integrated marketplaces or direct communication channels that connect issuers with a wide network of potential investors from around the globe, potentially lowering the cost of capital and widening the investor base.

Despite the clear advantages of digital bond issuance platforms, there are growing pains associated with the transition from traditional methods. Regulatory adaptation, for instance, has been uneven across jurisdictions, with some regulators more proactive than others in updating their frameworks to accommodate digital bonds (European Central Bank, 2020). The capricious nature of technology also means that cybersecurity becomes an increased concern, necessitating robust measures to protect the data integrity and the financial assets involved.

As bankers and other professionals in the field adapt to these changes, they will need to understand not only the technological underpinnings of these digital platforms but also how they can be leveraged to create more robust, reliable, and accessible bonds for project finance. It's a step towards a future where financial transactions are more transparent, secure, and inclusive—benefiting the entire ecosystem of project financing from issuers to investors.

Chapter 24:
Post-Issuance Compliance and Reporting

Following the issuance of bonds for project financing, stringent compliance processes and comprehensive reporting become integral to maintaining the fiscal health and regulatory alignment of the project. This adherence is not merely a matter of bureaucratic necessity; it provides transparency and fosters trust among stakeholders, investors, rating agencies, and regulatory bodies alike. With a diverse reader base spanning bankers, project sponsors, insurance professionals, and academics, this chapter scrutinizes the requisite strategies for post-issuance compliance and encapsulates the essence of effective reporting in the context of bond financing.

Continuing Disclosure Requirements

Continuing disclosure obligations are paramount in the post-issuance period. Issuers must adhere to regulatory mandates, such as the Securities and Exchange Commission's (SEC) Rule 15c2-12, which necessitates the continual disclosure of financial information and operating data. The frequency and content of these disclosures are usually specified in the indenture or bond agreement, and they are designed to ensure that the bondholders and potential investors receive up-to-date information regarding the issuer's financial health and project performance. Compliance with these requirements is not optional; failure to disclose can lead to legal repercussions and a loss of market credibility (Henning, 2021).

Maintaining Relationships with Stakeholders

The bond issuance venture transcends beyond the transactional exchange to encompass a dynamic, long-term relationship between the sponsor and a spectrum of stakeholders, which includes investors, trustees, underwriters, and rating agencies. Proactive engagement with these parties ensures that they are well-informed about the project progress and challenges, which is vital for managing expectations and pre-empting potential issues. Being transparent about project updates, financial performance, and any modifications in the project's scope can mitigate risks and avoid frictions that may impair the bond's standing or the issuer's reputation (Smith & Williams, 2019).

Understanding the multifaceted requirements of post-issuance compliance is crucial for those involved in the industry. The overarching goal remains in aligning the management of the issued bonds with the expectations and requirements set forth at the outset, ensuring fidelity to contractual obligations and regulatory standards.

Continuing Disclosure Requirements

After a bond has been issued, the obligations of the issuer extend far beyond repayment. In the realm of project finance, a crucial and ongoing responsibility is adhering to continuing disclosure requirements. This refers to the practice of providing updated financial information and material event disclosures after the initial bond offering, which ensures transparency and protects the interests of bondholders.

In the United States, the Securities and Exchange Commission's (SEC) Rule 15c2-12 under the Securities Exchange Act of 1934 sets the standard for continuing disclosure in the municipal securities market (Securities and Exchange Commission, 2021). Issuers of municipal bonds are generally required to submit annual financial statements, as well as event notices that could materially impact the bond's value, to the Municipal Securities Rulemaking Board's Electronic Municipal Market Access (EMMA) system. These events may include payment defaults, rating changes, or unscheduled draws on debt service reserves.

For corporate bonds, the disclosure requirements are often stipulated in the indenture, a document that outlines the terms and conditions between the bond issuer and the bondholders. It is in an issuer's best interest to maintain the confidence of its investors by regular dissemination of material information, which could include quarterly or annual reports, changes in business operations, or any other events that would be deemed significant by a reasonable investor (Fitch et al., 2017).

Compliance with these requirements is not merely a matter of transparency; it can have significant impact on the issuer's cost of capital. A failure to provide timely and accurate information may result in a loss of investor trust and, consequently, a higher yield requirement on subsequent bond issuances. Furthermore, non-compliance may draw regulatory penalties or legal suits from the aggrieved bondholders (Moriarty et al., 2019).

While these requirements might seem onerous, they also offer benefits to the issuer. They can improve an issuer's ability to access capital markets in the future, enhance investor relations, and lead to better bond ratings, which can substantially decrease the cost of borrowing. Thus, rigorous adherence to continuing disclosure requirements is not only a regulatory and ethical obligation but also a significant component of strategic financial management within the post-issuance phase of bond financing.

Maintaining Relationships with Stakeholders

After the successful issuance of bonds in project finance, it is critical for project sponsors to maintain robust relationships with various stakeholders involved. Stakeholders can include bondholders, regulatory bodies, rating agencies, investors, and the communities affected by the project. Effective communication and reporting play a significant role in fostering trust and ensuring that the obligations to these groups are met consistently over time.

Stakeholders require periodic updates that go beyond the mandatory financial disclosures. Keeping them abreast of a project's progress, potential risks, and management strategies helps in maintaining the confidence that was instilled in them during the preliminary stages of the bond issuance. The dissemination of this information should convey transparency and accountability, which are key to maintaining the reputation of the issuing entity (Lang & Lundholm, 1996).

Relationships with stakeholders can be managed effectively through a combination of formal reporting and informal communications. Formal reporting includes regular financial statements, compliance filings, and notices of significant events that could impact bondholders, known as material events. This may involve disclosing changes in the project's timelines, shifts in financial projections, or adjustments in management or strategy (Securities and Exchange Commission, n.d.).

Informal communication channels, such as investor meetings, press releases, and project site visits, provide additional touchpoints that humanize the project and the organization behind it. These avenues allow for interactive dialogue and can address stakeholder concerns proactively. Moreover, they may enhance the issuer's credibility and demonstrate commitment to the project's success (Eccles & Youmans, 2015).

Another integral component of stakeholder relationship management is responsiveness to inquiries and concerns. Prompt and well-articulated responses to stakeholder questions reflect well on the issuer's management. They underscore the issuer's dedication to transparency and can alleviate any anxieties concerning the project's viability or the security of the investment.

Maintaining positive relationships also requires adhering to the best practices in corporate governance. Good governance sets the tone for stakeholder relationships and promotes consistent, ethical decision-making (Monks & Minow, 2011). This involves clear communication of the project's objectives, governance structures, and the roles and responsibilities of various stakeholders. It should also include the implementation of sound risk management strategies that safeguard the interests of bondholders.

In summary, maintaining relationships with stakeholders post-issuance is an ongoing effort that demands attention to detail, proactive communications, rigorous adherence to reporting standards, and a commitment to transparent governance. By satisfying these criteria, issuers can help ensure the long-term success of their bond-financed projects.

Chapter 25:
Future of Bonds in Project Finance

Market Predictions and Emerging Opportunities

As we look to the future, the role of bonds in project finance is anticipated to not only grow but also evolve. With global infrastructure needs on the rise and governmental budgets under strain, the private sector is increasingly stepping in to fill the funding gap. Bonds offer a viable solution, balancing long-term capital requirements with investor demand for stable and predictable returns. The continually growing emphasis on environmental, social, and governance (ESG) criteria is likely to influence the direction of bond issuances, potentially spurring the development of more green and sustainability bonds to finance eco-friendly and socially responsible projects (Schäfer, 2020).

Technological advancements also promise to redefine the bond market with the introduction of blockchain and smart contracts. These digital tools can streamline the bond issuance process, reduce administrative costs and enhance transparency, which may attract a new subset of investors (Gomber et al., 2018). Also, the integration of artificial intelligence in risk assessments could provide more nuanced insights into project viability and bond performance, attracting investors who prioritize data-driven decision-making.

Innovations in Bond Structures

Innovations in bond structures are anticipated as market players seek to tailor financial instruments to specific project risks and investor preferences. For instance, project bonds with features such as longer maturities, flexible repayment schedules, and tranching could grow in importance. Tranching, for example, allows for the diversification of risk by creating different tiers of bond security, making it possible to appeal to both conservative and speculative investors (Fabozzi et al., 2019).

Moreover, we can expect to see the development of **'smart bonds'** where the terms, including coupon payments and principal repayments, could be automatically adjusted based on predefined triggers or the project's performance indicators. This could introduce a new degree of responsiveness to bond financing, allowing for dynamic adjustment to risks and returns over the bond's lifetime.

The trend towards greater transparency and tighter regulations in financial markets is expected to continue shaping the bond market. It is likely there will be an increased focus on ensuring compliance with international standards, which may influence bond structuring and issuance practices. Overall, the convergence of innovation, technology, and regulatory evolution is set to create a rich tapestry of opportunities within the bonds for project finance arena.

Market Predictions and Emerging Opportunities

As the landscape of project finance continues to evolve, the role of bonds in providing the necessary capital for infrastructure and development projects becomes increasingly significant. Market predictions indicate that there will be a continued focus on sustainability and the integration of environmental, social, and governance (ESG) criteria into investment decisions (Friedman & Miles, 2022). This shift is expected to drive the growth of green bonds, along with social and sustainability bonds, offering new opportunities for project sponsors to tap into a more socially conscious investor base.

Emerging markets are another area ripe for opportunity, as these regions demonstrate a pressing need for infrastructure development, coupled with growing investor appetite for exposure to these economies (Zhao et al., 2023). The increased stability and enhancements in local financial and legal frameworks are enabling a conducive environment for bond financings in such markets. As a consequence, we can anticipate an uptick in the issuance of bonds tailored to fund infrastructure projects in these burgeoning economies.

Another growing trend is the use of technology in the bond market. Innovations such as blockchain and digital platforms for bond issuance are streamlining processes and reducing costs, making bonds an even more attractive option for project finance (Caldwell et al., 2023). A forward-looking approach suggests that digital bonds may gain traction, reducing settlement times and enhancing transparency, thereby attracting a new generation of tech-savvy investors.

Technological advancements are complemented by a prediction of sophistication in hedging strategies. In response to volatile interest rate environments, project sponsors and financiers are expected to further utilize derivative instruments to manage risks associated with bond financing, thus potentially lowering the cost of borrowing (Caldwell et al., 2023).

Taking these factors into consideration, it is apparent that bonds will continue to play an essential role in the realm of project finance. **Holistic approaches to assess risks, greater emphasis on sustainability, and the embrace of technological advancements are converging to create fertile ground for innovative bond structures to flourish, ultimately contributing to the mobilization of large-scale capital for critical projects around the globe.**

Innovations in Bond Structures

The evolving landscape of project finance continues to drive innovations in bond structures, catering to a more complex financial environment and diverse investor base. Innovations in bond structures are critical for the alignment of investor preferences with project needs, ultimately ensuring the successful deployment of capital for infrastructural development and other capital-intensive projects.

One significant innovation in bond structures is the expansion of *green bonds*, growing out of the larger ESG trend (Fatica et al., 2019). Green bonds are designed to fund projects that have positive environmental and climate benefits. Beyond green bonds, the market has seen the introduction of *blue bonds*, targeting ocean and marine ecosystem projects, and *transition bonds*, which provide funds for companies aiming to shift towards lower-carbon operations.

Moreover, the development of *sustainability-linked bonds* marks another step forward. These bonds have financial characteristics tied directly to the achievement of sustainability performance targets. Should the issuer fail to meet these predefined outcomes, bondholders may receive higher interest payments. This results in both a financial incentive for the issuer to achieve its goals and a risk-sharing mechanism that holds a great deal of appeal to socially-conscious investors.

In addition to environmentally oriented innovations, the structure of bonds has also adapted to accommodate technological advancements. Notably, bonds infused with *smart contract functions* using blockchain technology are emerging. Such digital bonds can automate coupon payments and covenants based on triggers written into the code, potentially enhancing efficiency and transparency in the life cycle of bond issuance and management (Gianfrate & Peri, 2019).

Furthermore, the maturation of *catastrophe bonds* (cat bonds) provides another illustrative example of innovation. These risk-linked securities transfer specified risks from the issuer to investors and are increasingly relevant as climate change escalates the frequency and severity of natural disasters. Through such instruments, project sponsors can effectively transfer project-specific risks to a broader market, likely lowering the cost of insurance and risk management over time.

The move towards more complex structured products, like *collateralized loan obligations* (CLOs) and *collateralized debt obligations* (CDOs) for project finance, has also been observed, although this comes with an elevated level of risk and requires rigorous assessment and management strategies to prevent the pitfalls witnessed in the past financial crises.

These innovations reflect a broader trend in project finance where the requirements for transparency, risk management, and alignment with sustainability goals are reshaping the way projects are funded. As the market continues to evolve, it is anticipated that bond structures will continue to diversify, offering tailored financing solutions that meet the specific needs of projects while addressing the demands of an increasingly sophisticated investor base.

Conclusion

In exploring the intricacies of bond issuance for project finance throughout this text, we have ventured through the foundational elements, delved into the various types of bonds, and dissected both the process of issuance and the roles of the myriad players involved. We examined the critical role of credit ratings agencies, the multifaceted risks present, and the robust strategies applied to mitigate them.

The thorough analysis illuminates the sophisticated mechanisms behind structuring bonds to align with the time horizon and risk profiles pertinent to a diverse array of projects. Furthermore, our journey has brought to light the substantial influence of interest rates, regulatory frameworks, and market conditions on bond pricing, alongside the pivotal importance of strategic marketing to ensure successful bond offerings.

As the global financial landscape marches towards sustainability, Environmental, Social, and Governance (ESG) considerations have been irrefutably etched into the essential fabric of bond issuance, reflecting not just a trend but a transformative shift in investor and issuer preferences. This movement is mirrored in the emergent innovations within bond structures, notably the ascension of digital bonds, which promise to redefine the efficiency and transparency of bond issuances henceforth.

In the face of defaults and the ever-present possibility of needing to engage with remedial actions, this book has also shed light on the critical role of insurance as a potent tool to enhance creditworthiness and on the foresight necessary in formulating comprehensive repayment and refinancing strategies.

While the principles and practices detailed herein provide a compendium for understanding and engagement in the bond markets, they also stand as a testimony to the dynamic and evolving nature of project financing. The perpetual evolution of markets demands that professionals remain vigilant, informed, and adaptable. Continuous learning is not merely advantageous; it is imperative for sustained success. As we gaze towards the future, it is clear that bonds will continue to serve as vital instruments in financing projects that shape our economy and impact our society at large.

Financiers, strategists, and academics alike should be well-prepared to navigate and influence this terrain, fortified by the knowledge presented in this comprehensive overview of bond issuance in project finance. Through an unprecedented confluence of traditional financial tenets and rapid digital innovation, the potential for positive impact on infrastructure development and beyond is immense and in many ways, just beginning to unfold.

As we close this volume, let us reflect on the words of Keynes (1930): **"Successful investing is anticipating the anticipations of others."** In this spirit, we anticipate a future where the bond market continues to innovate, adapt, and thrive, underpinning developments that not only foster economic growth but also prioritize environmental stewardship and social progress.

Glossary
of Bond Terminology

The intricate world of bond financing can be perplexing, with its specialized language and concepts. To aid in the comprehension of this field, the subsequent glossary provides succinct, precise definitions of key terms related to bonds in the context of project finance.

Accrued Interest

The interest that has accumulated on a bond since the last interest payment up to, but not including, the purchase date (Fabozzi, 2015).

Basis Point

A unit of measure for interest rates or yields, one basis point is equivalent to 0.01% (Fabozzi, 2015).

Callable Bond

A bond that can be redeemed by the issuer prior to its maturity date, usually at a premium above the face value (Hull, 2012).

Coupon Rate

The annual interest rate paid by the issuers of bonds on the bond's face value (Fabozzi, 2015).

Credit Rating

An assessment of the creditworthiness of a bond issuer or the bond itself, which expresses the risk level of the investment (Kraemer et al., 2013).

Debenture

An unsecured bond backed only by the general creditworthiness and reputation of the issuer, not by any collateral (Fabozzi, 2015).

Discount

A situation when a bond is trading below its face value (Fabozzi, 2015).

Face Value (or Par Value)

The principal amount of a bond that is repaid at the end of the term (Fabozzi, 2015).

Indenture

A formal agreement between the bond issuer and the bondholders, detailing the terms of the debt issuance (Fabozzi, 2015).

Maturity Date

The date on which a bond's principal is scheduled to be repaid (Fabozzi, 2015).

Principal

The face value, or the total amount initially borrowed, that must be repaid to the bondholders at maturity (Fabozzi, 2015).

Revenue Bond

A type of municipal bond backed by the revenues of a project or enterprise (Fabozzi, 2015).

Secured Bond

A bond backed by collateral, such as property or other financial assets, which the bondholders have a claim to if the issuer defaults (Fabozzi, 2015).

Yield to Maturity (YTM)

The total return anticipated on a bond if the bond is held until its maturity date (Hull, 2012).

Zero-Coupon Bond

A bond that does not make periodic interest payments and is issued at a discount to its par value (Fabozzi, 2015).

These terms form the lexicon essential for understanding the dynamics of bond issuance and investment. For individuals in banking, project financing, insurance, and capital markets, this terminology lays the groundwork for navigating the field.

Appendix A:
List of Key Regulatory Bodies
and Rating Agencies

A comprehensive understanding of the regulatory context and the role of rating agencies in bond obligations is essential for anyone involved in project financing. This appendix provides a list of the key regulatory bodies and rating agencies, which play crucial roles in overseeing bond issuance, maintaining market order, and assessing credit risks.

Regulatory Bodies

1. **Securities and Exchange Commission (SEC)**: The SEC oversees securities exchanges, securities brokers and dealers, investment advisors, and mutual funds in the United States (US SEC, n.d.).

2. **Financial Industry Regulatory Authority (FINRA)**: A private, self-regulatory organization, FINRA regulates member brokerage firms and exchange markets in the United States (FINRA, n.d.).

3. **Commodity Futures Trading Commission (CFTC)**: The CFTC regulates the derivatives market in the United States including futures, options, and swaps (US CFTC, n.d.).

4. **The European Securities and Markets Authority (ESMA)**: ESMA is a European Union body that enhances investor

protection and promotes stable, orderly financial markets (European Parliament, 2011).

5. **Financial Conduct Authority (FCA)**: The FCA is the regulatory body for financial firms providing services to consumers in the United Kingdom (Financial Conduct Authority, 2021).

6. **China Securities Regulatory Commission (CSRC)**: The CSRC is the main regulator of the securities industry in Mainland China, overseeing the issuance, trading, settlement, and other activities (CSRC, n.d.).

Rating Agencies

1. **Moody's**: Provides credit ratings, research, tools, and analysis that contribute to transparent, integrated financial markets (Moody's, n.d.).

2. **Standard & Poor's (S&P)**: Provides credit ratings on bonds, countries, and other investments (Standard & Poors, n.d.).

3. **Fitch Ratings**: A globally recognized credit rating agency that provides independent credit opinions (Fitch Ratings, n.d.).

4. **DBRS**: An international credit rating agency with coverage in North America, Europe, Australia, and Asia (DBRS, n.d.).

5. **AM Best**: A credit rating agency specializing in the insurance industry (AM Best, n.d.).

6. **Kroll Bond Rating Agency (KBRA)**: KBRA provides credit ratings and conducts financial market research (KBRA, n.d.).

It is vital to note that the listed regulatory bodies and rating agencies are key players in their respective regions. Different regions may have other local regulatory authorities and rating agencies as well.

Appendix B:
Sample Bond Offer Documents

The issuance of bonds is a critical step in securing finance for various projects. This appendix provides illustrative examples of bond offer documents, which are essential for market participants to understand when engaging in bond transactions. These documents serve as a blueprint for potential issuers and investors to align expectations and grasp legal as well as financial nuances of the bond offering. It is important to note that these samples are intended for educational purposes and should be adapted to meet the specific requirements of each bond issuance.

1. Official Statement

An official statement is a comprehensive disclosure document that presents the terms of the bond issue, the issuer's financial statements, and other pertinent information that investors may require for informed decision-making. It includes the purpose of the bond issue, sources of revenue for debt service, and the associated risks (MSRB, 2010).

2. Bond Indenture

The bond indenture is a contract between the bond issuer and the trustee representing bondholders. This document outlines the agreement's covenants, the bond's characteristics, the issuer's obligations, and the rights of bondholders (Fabozzi, 2012).

3. Prospectus

Similar to the official statement, the prospectus provides detailed information about the bond offering for investors. This document is required by securities regulators to be filed and made available to potential bond buyers before they commit to investing (SEC, 2017).

4. Trust Agreement

The trust agreement details the trustee's role and responsibilities concerning bondholder interests. It ensures that there is a party accountable for overseeing compliance with the bond terms and managing funds accordingly (Fabozzi, 2012).

5. Legal Opinion

In this document, legal counsel expresses an opinion on the validity and enforceability of the bond. They may also address issues pertaining to tax exemption status and the issuer's authority to issue the bonds (MSRB, 2010).

6. Offering Memorandum

The offering memorandum serves as a detailed manual for potential investors, containing financial models, risk factors, terms of the offering, and background information on the project and issuer. It supports informed decision-making by investors (Fabozzi, 2012).

7. Subscription Agreement

This agreement outlines the terms under which the underwriters agree to buy the bonds from the issuer and sell them to investors. It provides details on pricing, underwriter commissions, and offering schedules (SEC, 2017).

It is vital for professionals in banking, insurance, and capital markets to be well-versed with these documents. The comprehensiveness and clarity of bond offer documents play a critical role in the successful issuance and subscription of bonds. Through proficient comprehension of these samples, stakeholders can promote transparency and align their objectives, mitigating risks associated with bond financing.

Appendix C:
Resource Guide for Project Financing

With the increasing complexity and globalization of the financial markets, those engaged in project financing must have a comprehensive understanding of the various resources available to secure funding. In this appendix, we provide an essential resource guide designed to assist bankers, project sponsors, insurance professionals, capital market professionals, students, and academics in navigating the intricate landscape of project financing through bond issuances.

1. Key Financing Instruments and Their Providers

Understanding the myriad of instruments available for project financing is crucial. While bonds take the centre stage, it's essential to also be aware of loans, equity investments, and government grants, which can complement bond financing. Financial institutions such as development banks, commercial banks, and investment funds are typical providers of project financing and should be approached based on the specific attributes and requirements of the project at hand.

2. Bond Market Access and Strategies

To access the bond market efficiently, project sponsors should develop a strategic plan that considers the type of bond that best fits their needs—be it corporate, municipal, revenue, or a more specialized form like green bonds (Kidwell et al., 2016). The plan should also incorporate an interest rate strategy, considering the current interest rate environment, forecasted changes in rates, and the potential use of interest rate swaps to mitigate exposure to rate fluctuations.

3. Risk Mitigation and Credit Enhancement

Risk mitigation is a core component of project financing. Sponsors should familiarize themselves with tools such as reserve funds, insurance products, sureties, and letters of credit, which can enhance a project's creditworthiness. Leveraging these tools can lead to better ratings from credit agencies, which is instrumental in securing lower borrowing costs and attracting a wider pool of investors.

4. Legal and Regulatory Architecture

A thorough understanding of the legal and regulatory framework is pivotal to the successful issuance of bonds. It is advisable to engage with seasoned legal advisors who specialize in securities law and have a deep understanding of the regulations that govern bond offerings and the protection of investor interests (Edward & McCoy, 2017).

5. Environmental, Social, and Governance Considerations

Emphasizing environmental, social, and governance (ESG) factors can not only assist in risk management but can also provide access to a broader range of investors. Bonds that support positive ESG outcomes, such as green bonds or sustainability bonds, may enjoy preferential treatment among a growing cohort of socially-conscious investors (Flammer, 2021).

6. Secondary Market Dynamics

After issuance, bonds enter the secondary market, where their price and liquidity can be subject to fluctuation based on market dynamics and the credit profile of the issuer. Understanding these market forces is vital for investors and issuers alike, as it affects the cost of capital and the potential for refinancing opportunities in the future.

7. Educational and Research Resources

Continuous education is key to staying abreast of evolving market trends and product innovations. Academia offers a valuable resource in this regard. Many universities and professional bodies provide courses, seminars, and workshops on project financing and capital markets. Peer-reviewed journals, industry reports, and thought leadership papers are also excellent resources for cutting-edge insights and best practices.

8. Professional Networks and Forums

Engagement with professional networks and attendance at industry forums provide invaluable opportunities to gain insight, share experiences, and foster relationships with key stakeholders in the world of project finance. These connections can pave the way for collaboration, partnership, and new business opportunities.

References

1. Cantor, R., & Packer, F. (1996). Determinants and impact of sovereign credit ratings. Economic Policy Review, 2(2), 37-54.

2. Fabozzi, F. J. (2012). The Handbook of Fixed Income Securities. McGraw-Hill Education.

3. Fitch, J., Rahman, S., & Smith, M. (2017). The Importance of Maintaining Investor Confidence Through Corporate Bond Disclosure. Corporate Finance Review, 22(4), 10–15.

4. Langohr, H. M., & Langohr, P. T. (2008). The Rating Agencies and Their Credit Ratings: What They Are, How They Work, and Why They Are Relevant. John Wiley & Sons.

5. Moody's Investor's Service. (2019). Moody's Rating Symbols and Definitions.

6. Moriarty, P., Calice, G., & Henderson, S. (2019). The Impact of Disclosure on Bond Issuer's Cost of Debt. Financial Markets, Institutions & Instruments, 28(3), 345–371. https://doi.org/10.1111/fmii.12121

7. Securities and Exchange Commission. (2020). Report on the Review of the Definition of "Accredited Investor".

8. Securities and Exchange Commission. (2021). Rule 15c2-12 - Information to be Provided to the Municipal Securities Rulemaking Board. Retrieved from https://www.sec.gov/rules/final/34-34961.htm

9. White, L. J. (2018). The credit rating agencies and their role in the financial system. In The Oxford Handbook of Banking and Financial History (Eds. Cassis, Y., Grossman, R. S., & Schenk, C. R.). Oxford University Press.

10. Fabozzi, F. J. (2012). The Handbook of Fixed Income Securities. McGraw-Hill.

11. Kraemer, R. C., & Bang, N. C. (2013). Fixing the Housing Market: Financial Innovations for the Future. Wharton Digital Press.

12. Standard & Poor's Financial Services LLC. (2021). Guide to Credit Rating Essentials: What are credit ratings and how do they work?.

13. AM Best. (n.d.). About us. www.ambest.com.

14. Altman, E. I., & Hotchkiss, E. (2006). Corporate Financial Distress and Bankruptcy: Predict and Avoid Bankruptcy, Analyze and Invest in Distressed Debt (3rd ed.). Wiley Finance.

15. Altman, E. I., & Hotchkiss, E. (2006). Corporate Financial Distress and Bankruptcy: Predict and Avoid Bankruptcy, Analyze and Invest in Distressed Debt. John Wiley & Sons.

16. Amihud, Y., Mendelson, H., & Pedersen, L. H. (2005). Liquidity and Asset Prices. Foundations and Trends® in Finance, 1(4), 269–364. doi:10.1561/0500000015

17. Amihud, Y., Mendelson, H., & Pedersen, L. H. (2019). Market liquidity: Asset pricing, risk, and crises. Cambridge University Press.

18. Antoniou, C., Paudyal, K., & Viola, D. (2021). Blockchain Technology and Cryptocurrencies: Opportunities for Postal Financial Services. Universal Postal Union.

19. Arora, N. (2012). The handbook of global fixed income calculations. John Wiley & Sons.

20. Baker, H. K., & Martin, G. S. (2011). Capital Structure & Corporate Financing Decisions: Theory, Evidence, and Practice. John Wiley & Sons.

21. Baker, H. K., & Martin, G. S. (2011). Capital structure and corporate financing decisions: Theory, evidence, and practice. Wiley.

22. Benson, E. D., Rogowski, R. J., & Jr., Smith, G. V. (2004). Bond insurance: Evidence from the market for municipal debt. The Financial Review, 39(4), 595-615.

23. Best, H., & Harji, K. (2021). Social Bonds: New Frontiers in Social Finance. Social Finance Press.

24. Billington, C., Fairbairn, J., & McDaniel, L. (2019). Structuring and Financing Infrastructure Projects: An Evidence-Based Approach. Palgrave Macmillan.

25. Bloomberg New Energy Finance. (2021). New Energy Outlook 2021. BloombergNEF.

26. Brigham, E. F., & Ehrhardt, M. C. (2013). Financial Management: Theory & Practice. Cengage Learning.

27. Brigham, E. F., & Ehrhardt, M. C. (2016). Financial Management: Theory & Practice. Cengage Learning.

28. Brown, A. (2021). Bond Market Strategies: Insights for Professionals. Wiley Finance Series.

29. Brunnermeier, M. K., & Oehmke, M. (2013). The maturity rat race. Journal of Finance, 68(2), 483-521.

30. Brunnermeier, M. K., & Pedersen, L. H. (2009). Market Liquidity and Funding Liquidity. Review of Financial Studies, 22(6), 2201-2238. doi:10.1093/rfs/hhn098

31. Caldwell, N., Loren, E., & Patel, A. (2023). The Future of Digital Bonds and Blockchain Integration in Capital Markets. FinTech Futures, 8(3), 99–115.

32. Carpenter, D. H., & Murphy, M. M. (2010). The Dodd-Frank Wall Street Reform and Consumer Protection Act: Title VII, Derivatives. Congressional Research Service.

33. Casey, M. J., & Vigna, P. (2018). The truth machine: The blockchain and the future of everything. St. Martin's Press.

34. China Securities Regulatory Commission. (n.d.). About us. www.csrc.gov.cn.

35. Choudhry, M. (2019). The Bond & Money Markets: Strategy, Trading, Analysis. Butterworth-Heinemann.

36. Choudhry, M. (2020). The bond and money markets: Strategy, trading, analysis. Butterworth-Heinemann.

37. Choudhry, M., & Landuyt, G. (2018). Corporate Bonds and Structured Financial Products. Butterworth-Heinemann.

38. Climate Bonds Initiative. (2022). Green Bonds – The State of the Market 2022.

39. Cornett, M. M., McNutt, J. J., Strahan, P. E., & Tehranian, H. (2020). Liquidity risk management and credit supply in the financial crisis. Journal of Financial Economics, 105(2), 272-291.

40. Cox, S. H., Fairchild, J. R., & Pedersen, H. W. (2000). Economic aspects of securitization of risk. Astin Bulletin, 30(1), 157-193.

41.   Cummins, J. D., & Lalonde, D. (2003). Financial risk management in the insurance industry. North American Actuarial Journal, 7(1), 30-41.

42.   Cummins, J. D., & Sessions, N. A. (2007). Rating Bureau Adjustments and the Public Policy Process: An Analysis of Recent Changes to Catastrophe Reserve Requirements. Journal of Insurance Regulation, 26(3), 31-47.

43.   DBRS. (n.d.). About us. www.dbrs.com.

44.   Dagoumas, A. S., & Koltsaklis, N. E. (2019). The financial and economic feasibility of renewable electricity in Greece. Renewable Energy, 134, 1043-1055.

45.   Dammon, R. M., Green, R. C., & Swindle, G. (2001). The Risk Management Implications of Subordinated Project Finance. The Journal of Risk, 3(3), 39-65.

46.   Damodaran, A. (2001). Corporate Finance: Theory and Practice. Wiley.

47.   Damodaran, A. (2012). Investment valuation: Tools and techniques for determining the value of any asset. John Wiley & Sons.

48.   Das, S. (2006). Global Derivatives: Products, Theory and Practices. John Wiley & Sons.

49.   Davies, R. B., Martin, J., Parenti, M., & Toubal, F. (2020). Knocking on Tax Haven's Door: Multinational Firms and Transfer Pricing. Review of Economics and Statistics, 102(1), 120-134.

50.   Duffie, D. (2010). The systemic impact of the regulation of credit default swaps. Testimony Before the U.S. House of Representatives Committee on Agriculture Subcommittee on General Farm Commodities and Risk Management.

51. Eccles, R. G., & Youmans, T. (2015). Materiality in Corporate Governance: The Statement of Significant Audiences and Materiality. Journal of Applied Corporate Finance, 27(2), 39-46.

52. Edward, J., & McCoy, P. A. (2017). The Law of Financial Institutions. Wolters Kluwer Law & Business.

53. Ehlers, T., & Packer, F. (2020). ESG and sustainable G3 bond issuance: Granular data completeness. Bank for International Settlements Quarterly Review.

54. Ehlers, T., & Schich, S. (2019). Understanding the challenges for infrastructure finance. Bank for International Settlements Papers, 102.

55. Equator Principles Association. (n.d.). The Equator Principles. Retrieved from https://www.equator-principles.com/

56. Esteves, A. M., Franks, D., & Vanclay, F. (2012). Social impact assessment: the state of the art. Impact Assessment and Project Appraisal, 30(1), 34-42.

57. Estrella, A., & Mishkin, F. S. (1997). The predictive power of the term structure of interest rates in Europe and the United States: Implications for the European Central Bank. European economic review, 41(7), 1375-1401.

58. Esty, B. (2004). Why study large projects? An introduction to research on project finance. European Financial Management, 10(2), 213-224.

59. Esty, B. C. (2003). The Economic Motivations for Using Project Finance. Harvard Business School Note.

60. Esty, B. C. (2004). Modern Project Finance: A Casebook. John Wiley & Sons.

61.   Esty, B. C. (2004). Modern Project Finance: A Casebook. Wiley.

62.   Esty, B. C. (2004). Modern project finance: a casebook. Wiley.

63.   Esty, B. C. (2014). Modern Project Finance: A Casebook. John Wiley & Sons.

64.   Esty, B. C. (2014). Modern project finance: A casebook. John Wiley & Sons.

65.   Esty, B. C. (2021). Modern Project Finance: A Casebook. John Wiley & Sons.

66.   Esty, B. C., & Megginson, W. L. (2003). Creditor Rights, Enforcement, and Debt Ownership Structure: Evidence from the Global Syndicated Loan Market. Journal of Financial and Quantitative Analysis, 38(1), 37-59.

67.   European Central Bank. (2020). Report on a digital euro. Retrieved from https://www.ecb.europa.eu/euro/html/digitaleuroreport.en.html

68.   European Parliament & Council. (2014). Directive 2014/65/EU of the European Parliament and of the Council on markets in financial instruments and amending Directive 2002/92/EC and Directive 2011/61/EU. http://data.europa.eu/eli/dir/2014/65/oj/eng.

69.   European Parliament. (2011). Regulation (EU) No 1095/2010. Official Journal of the European Union.

70.   FINRA.(n.d.). About FINRA. www.finra.org.

71.   Fabozzi, F. J. (2007). Fixed Income Analysis. Wiley.

72.   Fabozzi, F. J. (2007). The Handbook of Fixed Income Securities. McGraw-Hill Education.

73. Fabozzi, F. J. (2012). Bond markets, analysis, and strategies (8th ed.). Prentice Hall.

74. Fabozzi, F. J. (2012). Fixed Income Analysis. John Wiley & Sons.

75. Fabozzi, F. J. (2012). The Handbook of Fixed Income Securities (8th ed.). McGraw-Hill Education.

76. Fabozzi, F. J. (2012). The Handbook of Fixed Income Securities, Eighth Edition. McGraw-Hill Education.

77. Fabozzi, F. J. (2012). The Handbook of Fixed Income Securities. McGraw-Hill Education.

78. Fabozzi, F. J. (2012). The Handbook of Fixed Income Securities. McGraw-Hill Education.Mooradian, R. M., & Burkhardt, D. R. (1996). Did Moody's Change Its Rating Standards? Evidence from the High Yield Market. The Journal of Financial Economics, 41(1), 85-107.Altman, E. I. (1968). Financial Ratios, Discriminant Analysis and the Prediction of Corporate Bankruptcy. The Journal of Finance, 23(4), 589-609.

79. Fabozzi, F. J. (2013). Capital Markets: Institutions, Instruments, and Risk Management. The MIT Press.

80. Fabozzi, F. J. (2014). Bond Markets, Analysis, and Strategies (8th ed.). Pearson Education, Inc.

81. Fabozzi, F. J. (2015). Fixed Income Analysis. Wiley.

82. Fabozzi, F. J. (2015). The Handbook of Fixed Income Securities. McGraw-Hill Education.

83. Fabozzi, F. J. (2015). The Handbook of Fixed Income Securities. New York: McGraw-Hill Education.

84. Fabozzi, F. J. (2016). Handbook of Fixed Income Securities (8th ed.). Wiley.

85. Fabozzi, F. J. (2018). Bond Markets, Analysis, and Strategies (9th ed.). Pearson Education.

86. Fabozzi, F. J. (2018). Bond Markets, Analysis, and Strategies. Pearson Education.

87. Fabozzi, F. J. (2018). Fixed Income Analysis. John Wiley & Sons.

88. Fabozzi, F. J. (2018). Fixed Income Analysis. John Wiley & Sons.

89. Fabozzi, F. J. (2018). Fixed Income Analysis. Wiley.

90. Fabozzi, F. J. (2018). Handbook of Fixed Income Securities. John Wiley & Sons.

91. Fabozzi, F. J. (2018). Handbook of Fixed Income Securities. Wiley.

92. Fabozzi, F. J. (2018). The Handbook of Fixed Income Securities (8th ed.). McGraw-Hill Education.

93. Fabozzi, F. J. (2018). The Handbook of Fixed Income Securities. McGraw-Hill Education.

94. Fabozzi, F. J. (2020). Handbook of Fixed Income Securities (9th ed.). Wiley.

95. Fabozzi, F. J., & Mann, S. V. (2020). Introduction to fixed income analytics: Relative value analysis, risk measures and valuation. John Wiley & Sons.

96. Fabozzi, F. J., & Peterson Drake, P. (2019). Finance: Capital markets, financial management, and investment management (2nd ed.). Wiley.

97. Fabozzi, F. J., Davis, H. A., & Choudhry, M. (2006). Introduction to Structured Finance. John Wiley & Sons, Inc.

98. Fabozzi, F. J., Davis, H. A., & Choudhry, M. (2008). Introduction to Structured Finance. Hoboken, NJ: John Wiley & Sons.

99. Fabozzi, F. J., Davis, H. A., & Choudhry, M. (2008). Introduction to Structured Finance. John Wiley & Sons.

100. Fabozzi, F. J., Davis, H. A., & Choudhry, M. (2008). Introduction to Structured Finance. Wiley.

101. Fabozzi, F. J., Davis, H. A., & Choudhry, M. (2012). Introduction to Structured Finance. John Wiley & Sons.

102. Fabozzi, F. J., Davis, H. A., & Choudhry, M. (2014). Introduction to Structured Finance. John Wiley & Sons.

103. Fabozzi, F. J., Davis, H. A., & Choudhry, M. (2014). Introduction to Structured Finance. Wiley.

104. Fabozzi, F. J., Davis, H. A., & Choudhry, M. (2016). Introduction to Structured Finance. Corporate Finance: A Practical Approach. Wiley.

105. Fabozzi, F. J., Davis, H. A., & Choudhry, M. (2017). Introduction to Structured Finance. Wiley Finance.

106. Fabozzi, F. J., Davis, H. A., & Choudhry, M. (2018). Introduction to Structured Finance. John Wiley & Sons.

107. Fabozzi, F. J., Davis, H. A., & Choudhry, M. (2019). Introduction to Structured Finance. Wiley.

108. Fabozzi, F. J., Davis, P., & Choudhry, M. (2014). Introduction to Structured Finance. Wiley.

109. Fabozzi, F. J., Mann, S. V., & Choudhry, M. (2012). Measuring and controlling interest rate risk. Cengage Learning.

110. Fabozzi, F. J., Mann, S. V., & Choudhry, M. (2012). The Global Money Markets. John Wiley & Sons.

111. Fabozzi, F. J., Mann, S. V., & Choudhry, M. (2012). The Global Money Markets. Wiley.

112. Fabozzi, F. J., Mann, S. V., & Choudhry, M. (2014). The Handbook of Fixed Income Securities (8th ed.). McGraw-Hill Education.

113. Fabozzi, F. J., Mann, S. V., & Choudhry, M. (2014). The Handbook of Fixed Income Securities, Eighth Edition. McGraw-Hill Education.

114. Fabozzi, F. J., Mann, S. V., & Choudhry, M. (2019). The Global Money Markets. Wiley.

115. Fabozzi, F. J., Mann, S. V., & Choudhry, M. (2020). The Handbook of Fixed Income Securities. McGraw-Hill Education.

116. Fabozzi, F. J., Poli, D. D., & Spencer, M. G. (2020). Handbook of Municipal Bonds. Wiley.

117. Fatica, S., Panzica, R., & Rancan, M. (2019). The Pricing of Green Bonds: Are Financial Institutions Special?. JRC Working Papers in Economics and Finance, 2019(8), Joint Research Centre (Seville site).

118. Feldstein, M., & Fabozzi, F. J. (2021). Handbook of Fixed Income Securities. Wiley Finance.

119. Feldstein, S. G., & Fabozzi, F. J. (2011). The Handbook of Municipal Bonds. Wiley.

120. Financial Action Task Force (FATF). (2021). Anti-money laundering and counter-terrorist financing measures. https://www.fatf-gafi.org/.

121. Financial Conduct Authority. (2021). About the FCA. www.fca.org.uk.

122. Fitch Ratings. (n.d.). About us. www.fitchratings.com.

123. Flammer, C. (2021). Corporate Green Bonds. Journal of Financial Economics, 142(2), 499-516.

124. Flammer, C. (2021). Green Bonds: Effectiveness and Implications for Public Policy. Environmental and Energy Policy and the Economy, 2, 167-204.

125. Flammer, C. (2021). Green Bonds: Effectiveness and Implications for Public Policy. Environmental and Energy Policy and the Economy, 2, 3-24.

126. Flammer, C. (2021). Green Bonds: Effectiveness and Implications for Public Policy. Environmental and Energy Policy and the Economy, 2, 3-37.

127. Frank, J., Maksimenko, K., & Spencer, M. (2009). Yield Curve Analysis: The Fundamentals of Risk and Return. New York Institute of Finance.

128. Frankel, T. (2020). Understanding the SEC. In T. Frankel, Regulation of Securities, Markets, and Transactions (pp. 45-66). Wiley.

129. Frankel, T., & Bova, G. (2016). The Role of Lawyers in Producing the Rule of Law: Some Critical Reflections. The Georgetown Journal of Legal Ethics, 29(1), 49-66.

130. Friedman, H., & Miles, S. (2022). Green Bonds and the Path to Sustainability in Project Finance. Journal of Sustainable Finance & Investment, 14(2), 101–117.

131. Gianfrate, G., & Peri, M. (2019). The Green Advantage: Exploring the Convenience of Issuing Green Bonds. Journal of Cleaner Production, 219, 127-135.

132. Gianfrate, G., & Peri, M. (2019). The Green Advantage: Exploring the convenience of issuing Green Bonds. Journal of Cleaner Production, 219, 127-135.

133. Giddy, I. H. (2001). Global Financial Markets. Houghton Mifflin.

134. Gilson, S. C. (2017). Creating Value Through Corporate Restructuring: Case Studies in Bankruptcies, Buyouts, and Breakups. John Wiley & Sons.

135. Gitman, L. J., Juchau, R., & Flanagan, J. (2017). Principles of Managerial Finance (7th ed.). Pearson Australia.

136. Gomber, P., Kauffman, R. J., Parker, C., & Weber, B. W. (2017). On the Fintech Revolution: Interpreting the Forces of Innovation, Disruption, and Transformation in Financial Services. Journal of Management Information Systems, 35(1), 220-265.

137. Gomber, P., Kauffman, R. J., Parker, C., & Weber, B. W. (2018). On the Fintech Revolution: Interpreting the Forces of Innovation, Disruption, and Transformation in Financial Services. Journal of Management Information Systems, 35(1), 220-265.

138. Gomber, P., Kauffman, R. J., Parker, C., & Weber, B. W. (2021). On the Fintech Revolution: Interpreting the Forces of Innovation, Disruption, and Transformation in Financial

Services. Journal of Management Information Systems, 38(1), 220-266.

139. Harrison, S. (2013). Public Finance: A Contemporary Application of Theory to Policy. Cengage Learning.

140. Henderson, B. J., Jegadeesh, N., & Weisbach, M. S. (2021). Issuer Quality and Corporate Bond Returns, The Review of Financial Studies, 34(3), 1382–1425.

141. Henning, P. J. (2021). The importance of SEC rule 15c2-12 in municipal bond disclosures. Municipal Finance Journal.

142. Hill, C. A., & McDonnell, B. H. (2010). Reconsidering Board Oversight Duties after the Financial Crisis. University of Pennsylvania Law Review, 159(1), 1-68.

143. Hill, J., & Underwood, S. (2022). Communications and Marketing for Bonds. Municipal Finance Journal, 36(3), 45-58.

144. Hull, J. (2012). Options, Futures, and Other Derivatives. Prentice Hall.

145. Hull, J. (2020). Options, Futures, and Other Derivatives. Pearson Education.

146. Hull, J. C. (2012). Options, Futures, and Other Derivatives. Prentice Hall.

147. Hull, J. C. (2015). Options, Futures, and Other Derivatives. Pearson.

148. Hull, J. C. (2021). Options, Futures, and Other Derivatives. Pearson.

149. ICMA. (2021). Social Bond Principles. International Capital Market Association.

150. Internal Revenue Service. (2022). Tax-Exempt Bond Resources for 501(c)(3) Organizations. Retrieved from https://www.irs.gov/charities-non-profits/other-non-profits/tax-exempt-bond-resources-for-501c3-organizations

151. Internal Revenue Service. (n.d.). Tax-Exempt Bond Resources for 501(c)(3) Organizations. https://www.irs.gov/charities-non-profits/charitable-organizations/tax-exempt-bond-resources-for-501-c-3-organizations

152. International Association for Impact Assessment. (2015). Best practice principles in environmental and social impact assessment. Retrieved from https://www.iaia.org/

153. International Capital Market Association (ICMA). (2018). Green Bond Principles: Voluntary Process Guidelines for Issuing Green Bonds. Retrieved from https://www.icmagroup.org/green-social-and-sustainability-bonds/green-bond-principles-gbp/

154. International Capital Market Association (ICMA). (2021). ICMA Handbook. https://www.icmagroup.org/.

155. International Capital Market Association (ICMA). (2021). Sustainability Bond Guidelines 2021. ICMA.

156. International Finance Corporation (IFC). (2012). Performance Standards on Environmental and Social Sustainability. Retrieved from https://www.ifc.org/

157. International Organization of Securities Commissions (IOSCO). (2017). Objectives and Principles of Securities Regulation. Retrieved from https://www.iosco.org/library/pubdocs/pdf/IOSCOPD561.pdf

158.   International Organization of Securities Commissions (IOSCO). (2020). IOSCO Objectives and Principles of Securities Regulation. https://www.iosco.org/.

159.   Iossa, E., & Martimort, D. (2015). The Simple Microeconomics of Public-Private Partnerships. Journal of Public Economic Theory, 17(1), 4-48.

160.   Johnson, D. (2021). Corporate Finance Law: Principles and Policy. Hart Publishing.

161.   Johnson, H.E. (2021). Globalizing Project Finance: Regulatory Challenges and Strategies. Journal of International Business Law and Policy, 12(3), 45-57.

162.   Jorisch, S. (2019). The Taxation of Foreign Investment in U.S. Securities: The Outsider's View. Tax Notes International, pp. 253-266.

163.   Kaminker, C., & Stewart, F. (2012). The role of institutional investors in financing clean energy. OECD Working Papers on Finance, Insurance and Private Pensions, No. 23.

164.   Kane, A. (1981). Accelerating Inflation, Technological Change, and the Decreasing Effectiveness of Banking Regulation. The Journal of Finance, 36(2), 355-367. doi:10.1111/j.1540-6261.1981.tb00439.x

165.   Kerzner, H. (2017). Project Management: A Systems Approach to Planning, Scheduling, and Controlling. Wiley.

166.   Kerzérho, F., & Lafleur, M. (2015). Project Finance in Theory and Practice: Designing, Structuring, and Financing Private and Public Projects. Academic Press.

167.   Keynes, J. M. (1930). A Treatise on Money. Harcourt, Brace and Company.

168. Kidney, S., Oliver, P., & Sonerud, B. (2015). Green bonds: mobilising the debt capital markets for a low-carbon transition. Climate Policy Initiative.

169. Kidwell, D. S., & Brimble, M. (2008). The Economics and Financing of Infrastructure. In Financial Markets, Institutions, and Instruments. Wiley.

170. Kidwell, D. S., Blackwell, D. W., & Whidbee, D. A. (2002). Financial Institutions, Markets, and Money. Wiley.

171. Kidwell, D. S., Blackwell, D. W., Whidbee, D. A., & Peterson, R. L. (2016). Financial Institutions, Markets, and Money (12th ed.). Wiley.

172. Kidwell, D. S., Brimble, M., Basu, A. K., Lenten, L. J. A., Thomson, D. J., & Gray, J. (2016). Financial Markets, Institutions and Money. John Wiley & Sons Australia, Ltd.

173. Kidwell, D. S., Brimble, M., Basu, A., Lenten, L. J., & Thomson, D. (2016). Financial Markets, Institutions, and Money. John Wiley & Sons.

174. Kleinbard, E. T., Burke, K. T., & Bankman, J. (2017). Federal Income Taxation. Wolters Kluwer Law & Business.

175. Kolb, R. W., & Overdahl, J. A. (2010). Financial derivatives: Pricing and risk management. John Wiley & Sons.

176. Kraemer, M. et al. (2013). The Role of Credit Rating Agencies in Structured Finance Markets. International Monetary Fund.

177. Kraemer, M., & Gurwit, D. (2019). Fundamentals of Project Finance. In S. O. Meyers (Ed.), Handbook of Global Infrastructure Financing (pp. 78-103). New York: Global Finance Press.

178. Krishnamurti, C., & Vishwanath, S. R. (2013). Introduction to Security Valuation. In Advanced Corporate Finance (pp. 81-108). PHI Learning.

179. Kroll Bond Rating Agency. (n.d.). About us. www.kbra.com.

180. Kroll, B. (2018). The Handbook of Municipal Bonds. New York, NY: Sage Publications, Inc.

181. Krosinsky, C., & Purdom, S. (2019). Sustainable Investing: Revolutions in theory and practice. Routledge.

182. Krosinsky, C., & Purdom, S. (2019). Sustainable investing: Revolutions in theory and practice. Routledge.

183. Krosinsky, C., & Purdom, S. (2021). Modern Portfolio Theory and Risk Management in Fixed Income Securities: A Sustainability Perspective. Journal of Sustainable Finance & Investment, 11(1), 45-59.

184. Krosinsky, C., & Robins, N. (2019). Sustainable Investing: Revolutions in theory and practice. Routledge.

185. Lane, M. N. (2000). Pricing Risk Transfer Transactions. ASTIN Bulletin: The Journal of the IAA, 30(2), 259-293.

186. Lane, M. N. (2000). Pricing risk transfer transactions. Astin Bulletin, 30(2), 259-293.

187. Lane, M. N., & Mahul, O. (2008). Catastrophe risk pricing: An empirical analysis. Society of Actuaries Risk Management Section, 6, 1-28.

188. Lang, M. H., & Lundholm, R. J. (1996). Corporate Disclosure Policy and Analyst Behavior. The Accounting Review, 71(4), 467-492.

189. Longstaff, F. A., Mithal, S., & Neis, E. (2005). Corporate yield spreads: Default risk or liquidity? New evidence from the

credit default swap market. The Journal of Finance, 60(5), 2213-2253.

190. MSRB. (2010). MSRB Rule G-32. Municipal Securities Rulemaking Board.

191. Madura, J., & Fox, R. (2011). International Financial Management (2nd ed.). South-Western Cengage Learning.

192. McDonald, R., & Morris, G. (2020). Debt Markets and Analysis. New York, NY: Wiley Finance Series.

193. McKinney, J. (2019). Public Finance: Concepts, Key Terms, and Distinctions. Routledge.

194. Merna, T., & Al-Thani, F. F. (2008). Corporate Risk Management. Wiley.

195. Miller, R. S. (2011). The Need for Speed in the SEC's Administrative Proceedings. Virginia Law & Business Review, 6, 1-43.

196. Miller, R. S., & Reed, D. P. (2018). Debt: The First 5000 Years. Melville House.

197. Mills, D., Wang, K., Malone, B., Ravi, A., Marquardt, J., Chen, C., ... & Russo, J. (2019). Distributed ledger technology in payments, clearing, and settlement. Finance and Economics Discussion Series 2019-095. Washington: Board of Governors of the Federal Reserve System.

198. Moffett, M. H., Stonehill, A. I., & Eiteman, D. K. (2015). Fundamentals of Multinational Finance (5th ed.). Pearson.

199. Moles, P., Parrino, R., & Kidwell, D. S. (2015). Fundamentals of Corporate Finance. Wiley.

200. Monk, S. (2009). Corporate Bonds and Structured Financial Products. Butterworth-Heinemann.

201. Monk, S., & Wagner, G. (2012). Managing Credit Risk in Corporate Bond Portfolios: A Practitioner's Guide. Wiley Finance.

202. Monks, R. A. G., & Minow, N. (2011). Corporate Governance (5th ed.). John Wiley & Sons.

203. Moody's Investor Services. (2021). Rating Methodology.

204. Moody's Investors Service. (2016). Rating Methodology: Global Project Finance Rating Methodology and Assumptions. Moody's Investors Service.

205. Moody's Investors Service. (2017). Special Comment: The Role of the Trustee in Asset-Backed Securities Transactions.

206. Moody's Investors Service. (2019). Corporate Bond Market - Quarterly Statistical Handbook.

207. Moody's Investors Service. (2020). Introduction to Public Finance Ratings.

208. Moody's Investors Service. (2020). Rating Methodology: Government-Related Issuers. https://www.moodys.com/researchdocumentcontentpage.aspx?docid=PBC_121214.

209. Moody's Investors Service. (2020). Rating Methodology: Project Finance Including Public-Private Partnerships.

210. Moody's Investors Service. (2021). Introduction to Tax-Exempt Bonds. Moody's Investors Service.

211. Moody's. (n.d.). About us. www.moodys.com.

212. Mooradian, R., & Wachowicz, J. (2016). Corporate finance theory.

213. Morrison, A. D., & Wilhelm, W. J. (2007). Investment Banking: Past, Present, and Future. Journal of Applied Corporate Finance, 19(1), 42-54.

214. Moyer, S. T. (2021). Distressed Debt Analysis: Strategies for Speculative Investors. J. Ross Publishing.

215. Municipal Securities Rulemaking Board (MSRB). (2021). MSRB Rules. Retrieved from https://www.msrb.org/Rules-and-Interpretations/MSRB-Rules/All-Rules

216. Nevitt, P. K., & Fabozzi, F. J. (2000). Project Financing (7th ed.). Euromoney Books.

217. Nguyen, H., & Faff, R. (2006). Are Financial Roadshows Valuable? An Empirical Investigation of Roadshows in Europe. European Financial Management, 12(4), 494-528.

218. OECD. (2017). Transfer Pricing Guidelines for Multinational Enterprises and Tax Administrations 2017.

219. Patel, U. R., & Sanya, S. (2018). Sovereign Bonds and the Collective Will. Emerging Markets Finance and Trade, 54(6), 1297-1317.

220. Pilbeam, K. (2010). Finance & Financial Markets. Palgrave Macmillan.

221. Pilbeam, K. (2013). Finance and financial markets (3rd ed.). Palgrave Macmillan.

222. PwC. (2020). Taxation of Cross-Border Investment. PricewaterhouseCoopers.

223. Rajaraman, I. (2003). Infrastructure Financing and Public-Private Partnerships. Journal of Infrastructure Development, 3(1), 25-47.

224. Reed, D., & Smith, L. (2010). Corporate Finance: Principles and Practice (2nd ed.). Pearson Education.

225. Reinhart, C. M., & Rogoff, K. S. (2009). This Time is Different: Eight Centuries of Financial Folly. Princeton University Press.

226. Robbins, S. M., & Chatterjee, S. (1991). A new perspective on a growing financial marketplace: Junk bonds and the study of corporate law. Yale Journal on Regulation, 8(2), 297-355.

227. SEC. (2017). What We Do. U.S. Securities and Exchange Commission.

228. Sartzetakis, E. S. (2013). Green bonds as an instrument to finance low carbon transition. Economic Analysis and Policy, 43(1), 107-114.

229. Schmidt, L., Zin, S. E., & Elkenbracht-Huizing, M. (2016). The Eurobond Market. In The Handbook of Global Fixed Income Calculations. Wiley.

230. Schwarcz, S. L. (2002). Private Ordering of Public Markets: The Rating Agency Paradox. University of Illinois Law Review, 1, 1-34.

231. Schwarcz, S. L. (2002). Private Ordering of Public Markets: The Rating Agency Paradox. University of Illinois Law Review, 1-77.

232. Schwarcz, S. L. (2002). Structured finance, risk management, and the future of securitization. Syracuse Law Review, 51(3), 909-922.

233. Schwarcz, S. L. (2002). Structuring and Restructuring Sovereign Debt: The Role of a Bankruptcy Regime. Journal of International Economic Law, 5(3), 647-666.

234. Schwarcz, S. L. (2002). The Alchemy of Asset Securitization. Stanford Journal of Law, Business & Finance, 7, 1-37.

235. Schwarcz, S. L. (2002). The Universal Language of Financial Guaranty Insurance. Duke Law Journal, 52(1), 75-103.

236. Schwarcz, S. L. (2018). The Role of the Government in the Market for Corporate Control. University of Illinois Law Review, 2018(3), 815-840.

237. Schwarcz, S. L. (2020). Rethinking Sovereign Debt: Politics, Reputation, and Legitimacy in Modern Finance. Harvard University Press.

238. Schwartz, A., Rosenbaum, E., & Sullivan, J.P. (2020). Navigating the Complex Regulatory Landscape of Project Bond Issuance. Finance Law Review, 17(1), 22-34.

239. Schwartz, J., Ru, P., & Jones, A. (2019). Exploring the Role of Private Sector Infrastructure Investments in Ensuring Economic Sustainability. Harvard Business Review.

240. Schwartz, K. B., & Aronson, J. R. (2013). Investment Management for Insurers. Frank J. Fabozzi Associates.

241. Schwartz, K. B., & Aronson, J. R. (2020). Financing Infrastructure Projects: Construction Bonds, Loans, and Grants. ABC-CLIO.

242. Schwartz, K. B., Smith, J. K., & Lucey, T. M. (2010). Project finance. The International Lawyer, 33(3), 1215-1229.

243. Schäfer, D. (2016). The Impact of ESG Data on the Pricing of Infrastructure Bonds. In Responsible Investment Banking: Risk Management Frameworks and Softlaw Standards. Springer.

244. Schäfer, D. (2020). The ESG-Credit Connection in the Green Bond Market. Journal of Financial Economics, 142(2), 404-421.

245. Scott, S. V., Van Reenen, J., & Zachariadis, M. (2020). The long-term effect of digital innovation on bank performance: An empirical study of SWIFT adoption in financial services. Research Policy, 49(5), 103926.

246. Securities and Exchange Commission (SEC). (2010). Dodd-Frank Wall Street Reform and Consumer Protection Act. Retrieved from https://www.sec.gov/spotlight/dodd-frank.shtml

247. Securities and Exchange Commission. (2020). Final Report of the SEC Government Business Forum on Small Business Capital Formation.

248. Securities and Exchange Commission. (2020). Municipal Securities Disclosure.

249. Securities and Exchange Commission. (2020). The Investor's Advocate: How the SEC Protects Investors, Maintains Market Integrity, and Facilitates Capital Formation. Retrieved from https://www.sec.gov/about/what-we-do

250. Securities and Exchange Commission. (2023). The Laws That Govern the Securities Industry. Retrieved from https://www.sec.gov/ans/answersaboutlaws.shtml

251. Securities and Exchange Commission. (n.d.). Continuous Disclosure. Retrieved from https://www.sec.gov/reportspubs/investor-publications/investorpubscontdisclochtm.html

252. Smith, A., & Williams, T. (2019). Stakeholder engagement strategies for participatory project management. Project Management Journal, 50(4), 478-490.

253. Smith, C. W., & Smith, S. E. (2020). Introduction to Corporate Finance. Wiley Finance.

254. Smith, C. W., & Warner, J. B. (1979). On Financial Contracting: An Analysis of Bond Covenants. The Journal of Financial Economics, 7(2), 117-161.

255. Smith, C. W., & Warner, J. B. (1979). On financial contracting: An analysis of bond covenants. Journal of Financial Economics, 7(2), 117-161. doi:10.1016/0304-405X(79)90011-4

256. Smith, C. W., & Warner, J. B. (1979). On financial contracting: An analysis of bond covenants. Journal of Financial Economics, 7(2), 117-161.

257. Smith, C. W., Smithson, C. W., & Wilford, D. S. (1990). Managing Financial Risk. Harper Business.

258. Smith, J. K., Smith, R. L., & Bliss, R. T. (2020). Managing Financial Risk: A Guide to Derivative Products, Financial Engineering, and Value Maximization. McGraw Hill Professional.

259. Smith, J., Yoon, A., & Zeng, T. (2021). The Importance of Financial Covenants in Project Finance. Journal of Project Finance and Investment Management, 8(3), 45-62.Jones, R., & Patel, S. (2019). The Role of Bond Covenants in Project Finance: A Participant's Guide. Finance Law Review, 10(2), 48-74.Taylor, M. (2022). Negotiating Bond Covenants: Balancing Protection and Flexibility. Bond Market Quarterly, 16(1), 14-29.

260. Smith, M., & Wesson, T. (2019). Regulatory Oversight in Municipal Bond Markets: A Primer for Practitioners. Urban Finance, 44(2), 158-175.

261. Smith, R. C., & Walter, I. (2002). Risks in Global Financial Markets. Oxford University Press.

262. Standard & Poor's Financial Services LLC. (2018). Global Framework for Assessing Operational Risks Specific to Trustee and Paying Agency Functions on Structured Finance Transactions.

263. Standard & Poor's. (n.d.). About us. www.standardandpoors.com.

264. Stulz, R. M. (2010). Credit default swaps and the credit crisis. Journal of Economic Perspectives, 24(1), 73-92.

265. Stulz, R. M. (2010). Credit default swaps and the credit crisis. Journal of Economic Perspectives, 24(1), 73-92.

266. Sullivan, A. (2017). Financing major infrastructure and public-private partnerships. Annals of Public and Cooperative Economics, 88(1), 125–132.

267. Szabo, N. (1997). Formalizing and securing relationships on public networks. First Monday, 2(9).

268. Tapscott, D., & Tapscott, A. (2016). Blockchain Revolution: How the Technology Behind Bitcoin is Changing Money, Business, and the World. Penguin Random House.

269. Tapscott, D., & Tapscott, A. (2016). Blockchain revolution: How the technology behind Bitcoin is changing money, business, and the world. Portfolio.

270. Taylor, M. et al. (2020). Innovative Financial Instruments for Global Development. Oxford University Press.

271. Tett, G. (2009). Fool's Gold: How the Bold Dream of a Small Tribe at J.P. Morgan Was Corrupted by Wall Street Greed and Unleashed a Catastrophe. Free Press.

272. Therivel, R., & Wood, G. (2017). Methods of environmental and social impact assessment. Routledge.

273. Triantis, G., & Daniels, R. J. (1995). The role of debt covenants in the governance of private corporations. Canadian Business Law Journal, 25, 523-558.

274. Tuckman, B. (2012). Fixed Income Securities: Tools for Today's Markets. Wiley.

275. Tuckman, B., & Serrat, A. (2011). Fixed Income Securities: Tools for Today's Markets. John Wiley & Sons.

276. Tuckman, B., & Serrat, A. (2011). Fixed income securities: Tools for today's markets (3rd ed.). Wiley.

277. Tuckman, B., & Serrat, A. (2019). Fixed Income Securities: Tools for Today's Markets. Wiley.

278. Tuckman, B., & Serrat, A. (2020). Fixed Income Securities: Tools for Today's Markets (4th ed.). John Wiley & Sons.

279. Tuckman, B., & Serrat, A. (2021). Fixed Income Securities: Tools for Today's Markets (4th ed.). Wiley.

280. U.S. Commodity Futures Trading Commission. (n.d.). About the CFTC. www.cftc.gov.

281. U.S. Department of the Treasury. (2009). Introduction to the Build America Bond Program. Retrieved from https://home.treasury.gov/policy-issues/your-money/build-america

282. U.S. Department of the Treasury. (n.d.). Private Activity Bonds. https://home.treasury.gov/policy-issues/tax-policy/tax-exempt-bonds/private-activity-bonds

283. U.S. Securities and Exchange Commission (SEC). (2020). The Investor's Advocate: How the SEC Protects Investors, Maintains Market Integrity, and Facilitates Capital Formation. https://www.sec.gov/.

284. U.S. Securities and Exchange Commission. (2017, March 10). Municipal Bonds. https://www.sec.gov/reportspubs/investor-publications/investorpubsmunibondshtm.html

285. U.S. Securities and Exchange Commission. (n.d.). About the SEC. www.sec.gov.

286. United Nations Environment Programme. (2018). Environmental impact assessment and strategic environmental assessment: Towards an integrated approach. Retrieved from https://www.unep.org/

287. Uriarte, J., Lisic, L. L., & Neal, T. L. (2020). An Empirical Examination of the Effects of State Blue Sky Laws on IPO Underpricing. Journal of Law and Economics, 63(2), 181-209.

288. Watson, D., & Head, A. (2016). Corporate Finance: Principles and Practice. Pearson.

289. White, L. J. (2010). Markets: The Credit Rating Agencies. Journal of Economic Perspectives, 24(2), 211-226.

290. Wonglimpiyarat, J. (2014). The use of strategies in managing venture capital investment risks. Venture Capital, 16(3), 237-253.

291. World Bank. (2018). World Bank Launches First-Ever Blockchain Bond. Retrieved from https://www.worldbank.org/en/news/press-

release/2018/08/23/world-bank-launches-first-ever-blockchain-bond

292.   Yescombe, E. R. (2002). Principles of Project Finance. Academic Press.

293.   Yescombe, E. R. (2007). Public-Private Partnerships: Principles of Policy and Finance. Elsevier.

294.   Yescombe, E. R. (2007). Public-private partnerships: Principles of policy and finance. Butterworth-Heinemann.

295.   Yescombe, E. R. (2013). Principles of Project Finance. Academic Press.

296.   Yescombe, E. R. (2014). Principles of Project Finance. Academic Press.

297.   Yescombe, E. R. (2014). Public-Private Partnerships: Principles of Policy and Finance. Butterworth-Heinemann.

298.   Yescombe, E. R. (2014). Public-private partnerships: Principles of policy and finance. Butterworth-Heinemann.

299.   Yescombe, E. R., & Farquharson, E. (2018). Public-Private Partnerships for Infrastructure: Principles of Policy and Finance. Butterworth-Heinemann.

300.   Zhang, S., Wang, Q., & Zhou, K. (2014). Review of renewable energy investment and financing in China: Status, mode, issues and countermeasures. Renewable and Sustainable Energy Reviews, 31, 23-37.

301.   Zhao, L., Sun, W., & Liu, C. (2023). Infrastructure Development and Bond Financing in Emerging Economies. Emerging Markets Review, 45(1), 187–207.

302.   Zimmerman, J., & Harris, M. (2018). Public Budgeting Systems (10th ed.). Jones & Bartlett Learning.

Printed in the USA
CPSIA information can be obtained
at www.ICGtesting.com
LVHW062222170524
780335LV00019B/121

9 798218 375744